SONG SO WILD
AND BLUE

SONG SO WILD AND BLUE

A LIFE WITH THE MUSIC
OF JONI MITCHELL

PAUL LISICKY

HarperOne

An Imprint of HarperCollins*Publishers*

HarperCollins books may be purchased for educational, business, or sales promotional use. For information, please email the Special Markets Department at SPsales@harpercollins.com.

FIRST EDITION

Designed by Nancy Singer

Library of Congress Cataloging-in-Publication Data has been applied for.

ISBN 978-0-06-328037-3

24 25 26 27 28 LBC 5 4 3 2 1

This book is for Jude.

AUTHOR'S NOTE

WHEN I FIRST CONCEIVED OF THIS PROJECT, A FRIEND SAID, WILL you interview Joni? Can I come along? Immediately, I knew it wasn't going to be that kind of book. I wanted the emphasis to be on Joni's songs, which have an independent life, and their influence on my creative work. It turned out it was impossible to think about the songs without at least gesturing toward their maker, and to how and why she would have written them. Sometimes, as I was writing, the line between Joni and me felt so thin that it nearly dissolved—whose mind was whose? Occasionally the book envisions Joni's perspective based on what I know of her life from her interviews, biographies, website, and songs. Those passages are tethered to facts.

This book is an act of imagination. A few names have been changed along the way to protect the privacy of individuals.

CONTENTS

SONG SO WILD
AND BLUE

G
A
T
H
E
R
I
N
G

DOWN TO YOU

~~~~~~~~

THE SMELL OF STRUCK NICKEL CAME UP FROM THE STRINGS. IT was already past four in the morning. She leaned into the shape of her new guitar, strumming a song she'd been working on, and while it was better to be playing an actual guitar versus her baritone ukulele, something was off, something about her knuckles—she couldn't make a firm D major chord. Her left hand hadn't moved the way she'd wanted it to, not since she had polio at nine, when she had to lie perfectly still in bed for weeks to limit the spread of the virus. She contorted her hand on the fingerboard. Every other guitarist she knew in her circles could play D major—why not her? She looked out the window of her Detroit apartment and imagined the voice of her mother, who liked to call her a quitter. The trick was to say no to the face that had mixed up love with control.

Where was that face when she reached for the tuning peg and twisted it beyond the expected rotation? Joni says she learned to retune from Eric Andersen, but he'd only suggested open G and D modals, tunings already common among folk and blues musicians. Joni didn't stop there. She didn't stop when the higher strings snapped and flailed, or when someone said, "That's no way to play a guitar; you're killing the neck." By retuning the instrument to the pitches that felt right, she could play the left-hand shapes that suited her fingers. She opened up the orchestral breadth of the guitar, deepening its bottom range, rewriting the rules of Western musical tradition. But who starts in the clouds? Like any artist, her task was to find a sound that captured how she talked, how the currents of her brain moved, how she held the wineglass in her hand as she walked from one side of the party to the other.

Retuning her guitar? Audacious as likening herself to van Gogh, Picasso, Beethoven, and Shakespeare. Audacious as hiring the musicians and firing them when necessary. How many men would she have to convince? She was on her own in a world of men, straight men, who must have crossed their arms over their chests, leaned back in their chairs, and looked at her with mildly amused contempt. *August night, runway lights. Plane landing, rubber on hot asphalt. Play that.*

By the time of *Court and Spark*, her sixth album, she'd grown tired of playing solo, and so many of the techniques she'd invented on her own were being questioned, challenged, dismissed by schooled musicians. One night, when she'd had enough, she taped a sign to the studio door: NO BOYS ALLOWED. Always telling her *You can't* before she'd even had the chance to explore. It killed everything to begin with that fear of failure.

The sixth string, the fifth string—when would she think her guitar had taken enough punishment? And those tunings went down through the years, hitting the ears of people along a cause-way, atop a skyscraper, in an underground cave. Magic, though there had to be a better word for it. Sorcery? *Hello, out there.* An astronaut. A drug dealer. A pilgrim.

So many strangers waiting to be transformed by her songs, though none of them knew that yet.

~~~~

The wind blew through the open window. Tonight I didn't mind that the Brooklyn trees were stripped of leaves, the light falling on their trunks in buttery gold. My new friend and I were DMing about music, our correspondence becoming more involved once it became clear that we were crazy about the same songs. It would have been too on the nose to talk about Joni, though he must have considered it. Joni was fraught territory. Joni was personal. And as far as questions: What if I was the kind of person who only listened to *Blue*? What if he dismissed everything before 1976 and believed she'd reached her pinnacle with *Hejira*? What if I hated the jazz work, or else loved it too much and wished she'd done more albums in the vein of *Mingus* but maybe with acoustic instruments rather than electronic? What if he believed there was such a thing as a single coherent Joni over time, and not a village of poets contradicting—or at least questioning—one another? What if I didn't know an open tuning from a corkscrew? What if he thought "The Circle Game" was utter genius? I mean, I loved the imaginary campfire of "The Circle Game," but painted ponies and cartwheels and being captive on a carousel?

It would be very easy to make an ending before there was a

beginning. Red flags—picture a grass slope stabbed with them, snapping in the wind. And if not red flags, polite acknowledgment, bland agreement, then—nothing. People could barely look after themselves. No one wanted connection these days. There were already too many reasons for awkwardness, especially on these things we call the apps and the socials.

And besides, who didn't love Joni these days? I rarely ran into a person who didn't admit to being a Joni fan or say, *My grandmother is a total Joni fan.* It came with no risk of bad taste, no chance of sounding a little dim, whether you were queer, straight, Black, brown, old, young, an academic, or someone who rung up blueberries and extension cords at the Dollar General on the edge of town. Everyone believed they had a personal stake in Joni's excellence, which wasn't always the story, and certainly not when I was in high school and my friends listened to Fleetwood Mac's *Rumours* as if it were the best thing to have ever arrived on Earth in the form of sound. To admit to loving Joni in the third decade of the third millennium was as fresh as saying you loved ice cream and lakes and storm windows and electric appliances.

Instead, Jude wrote to me about PJ Harvey, the British singer-songwriter. Certainly someone springing out of Joni's lineage, but likely to have complaints about her, as one inevitably does about one's parents, especially when they take up their fair share of the room with their feelings. I posted the song "When Under Ether" from *White Chalk*, and Jude wrote about PJ taking flak for her piano arrangements on the album, the instrument being a previously unexplored one for her. *I find the naïveté adds to the haunted feeling of the music,* he texted. *The reviewer got it wrong.* Then went on to quote from the piece itself, which was clueless in all expected risk-averse ways in that it elevated professional polish over capturing the process of a song coming into being. There wasn't judgment in Jude's tone. He wasn't shaking his fist. It was melancholy puzzlement that some people couldn't see a wonder when it was looking right at them with an open face.

His DM was more essay than casual comment, and by *essay*, I mean *crafted*, *animated*. It had *nouns*. There was no hint of power in its assessment. Instead, it said, *I'm going to show you, friend of spirit, something that you don't know about music, and maybe you're going to show me what you know too.*

I didn't reply for days. This wasn't coolness. My heart wasn't hard. In fact, I could be annoyed by acquaintances who behaved as if locking one's gates were the inevitable consequence of being out of a long relationship. I wasn't tired, nor was I fully allergic to the cycle of hope, expectation, taming expectation only to come down to smoke and ash. But honestly? In eleven years of single life, I'd taught myself, in increments, without being fully conscious of it, not to direct all my energy into one person—no small thing for someone who tended to *latch*. I had many friends: deep friends, casual friends, friends who were *more*. I had a rich and various and often frenetic life. I could walk into a crowded room by myself and stand at the center, and I didn't even care if anybody came up to talk or not, but inevitably they did, because it looked like I didn't need them. I'd built myself back up from scratch over the course of my fifties, even though others had contributed switches and lumber. I told myself I wasn't lonely, and I believed it—as many as six times a day. Why screw up such goodness? Though at the same time, I was astounded that I'd ended up here. I was walking down Court Street for the fifth time that afternoon, setting myself out on another pointless errand for a yellow key cover and Miracle-Gro. It exhausted me that, aside from my teaching, so much of my waking life was dependent on my *I*, that I had to put such effort into parenting this *I*, keeping this *I* involved and delighted, when I might have just rather looked at the person sitting in the chair across the room and said, *You need something, babe?*

When I finally wrote him a more involved note on his birthday, I texted, *You're so right about that reviewer missing the point. It seems to me that singer-songwriters use amateurism or SEARCHING to their advantage.* I knew I was actually talking about Joni's methodology but wasn't ready to go there just yet. Then let out a breath. *Just thinking of the dulcimer songs on* Blue. By that I meant Joni was learning the dulcimer as she wrote those songs; the constraint made them great.

Later, he told me he'd been biking the mountains of Northern Virginia with his brother, Luke, in the hour of that DM. Bike in the grass, light on his legs and on the backs of his hands. October, coming on Halloween.

In the days to come, I found out that he was a neurologist, musician, and writer. Found out that he was a dedicated reader of Shelley, James Tate, Yeats, and Lydia Davis. Found out that after years in Southern California, he'd moved back to Louisiana eighteen months into the pandemic to be a doctor in his hometown on the edge of the Atchafalaya Basin, just off the eighteen-mile bridge through the cypress swamp. But along with the exchange of our histories, we kept coming back to Joni as our orientation point: her phrasing, her tunings, her guitar versus her piano songs. Her half-baked songs—it felt both transgressive and thrilling to talk about the half-baked songs in such a way that made our disappointment bring us into a deeper form of respect. As to our favorites? It surprised us, and didn't, that with few exceptions, we shared the same list. "The Wolf That Lives in Lindsey," "Down to You," "Let the Wind Carry Me," "Same Situation," "Jericho," "Edith and the Kingpin," "Rainy Night House," "Blue."

When we talked more specifically about relationships, the long ones we'd been through, he said he valued sweetness. He said he wanted to be sweet to me.

At an earlier point in my life, I might have found a reason to be confused. Sweetness? What other man knew himself well enough not just to want sweetness but to say it aloud, without any shame? I had no inclination to be coupled again, but I wanted to get to know him—specifically him. He was very sexy to me, and that scared me.

I looked at his FaceTime face: olive eyes, thick beard, soulful expression that I thought of as the face of inquiry, a physical representation of one of Joni's angular chords. Did I say vascular arms? Long back? He looked like he could have come from the sixteenth century and stepped out of one of the portraits of El Greco, but with a face of affection, curiosity, mischief, blazing intelligence, and light.

~~~~~

It could have been "Woodstock," could have been "River." Could have been "Night Ride Home," "Otis and Marlena," "The Three Great Stimulants," "No Apologies"—any of the songs that are relatively straightforward, that move like other people's songs harmonically and melodically. Instead, the first video he sent was "Down to You," one of Joni's most demanding songs, one she'd rarely done in concert, probably because it was too difficult to make all its independent moving parts sync up. He didn't perform it for me—that would come a bit later. Instead, in the span of a minute, he offered a little lecture about its architecture, which isn't AABA like many popular songs, but ABA-cadenza-A. So much goes on in that cadenza, a morphing instrumental passage that takes direction from classical and jazz modalities, the bass note rarely acting as the root of the chord. It isn't the most romantic song. If anything, it is the opposite, in that its narrative considers the inevitable loneliness that comes from sex with strangers, with people you might pick up in a bar after you've had drinks. Joni doesn't overplay that loneliness, though the phrase "Love is gone" punctures the listener. That loss is no longer just personal in the second verse but societal. A breakdown of connection, a collapse of kindness and warmth, a cautionary take in a collection of songs about freedom, especially sexual freedom. Was Jude, like me, tired of an ongoing pursuit that seemed significant once, a catching-up after being taught by the culture that his sexuality didn't exist, his body didn't exist, and, if it did, his longing was depraved, a matter to be policed? Against that, what else was there but to fuck into one's reclaimed gorgeousness again and again?

He knew I was a fan of songwriting but didn't know that I had been a songwriter once, that I'd published music in my late teens and early twenties, that I had once wanted to write work that approached the intricacy of Joni's music. He didn't yet know that I had breathed and drank that desire, that everything else had been an obstacle to me. And that one day I had stopped. Well, if it had been one day, I'd have been kinder to myself and music. A proper mourning could have occurred. I could have wrapped music inside a baby blanket, sent that basket down the river as the voice inside went silent and disappeared among the reeds. I simply became more interested in prose writing. I turned to writing as if it were a new man standing on the opposite bank.

I'd come to think of my paragraphs as the sweet ghosts of my songs. I was a better writer for pulling in what I knew about phrasing, unexpected chordal leaps, shifts in meter, changes in emotional register, the silence between notes. Every writer should begin with another art form—acting, painting, sculpture—and use that as a point of comparison or departure. It was one of the few pronouncements I'd passed along to my writing students, and it was never a lie. But the way I talked about leaving music behind seemed easy, almost cozy, as if I'd simply knocked out a fireplace, pulled up the rotting floorboards in the kitchen, and basked in the sunlight through the windows around the table. By deciding to think of myself as a prose writer, I could say, *Here I can make something on my own and not have to deal with the complexities of others' egos, the perils that come with collaboration.* But it hadn't occurred to me that giving up music was as extreme as moving to the Mojave and giving up water in order to be a better person.

I missed the hammering of my fingers, missed taking satisfaction in their strength and reach. I missed worrying about the condition of my voice, whether that granular scratch meant strep throat or just the season of cedar pollen. I missed the sense of inhabiting my body that music gave me, locking myself in my neck, thighs, diaphragm, and butt in the manner of an athlete. I missed trying to impress someone by simply singing and playing for them, a practice that somehow took on a life of its own in that my ego dissolved and we were water. Music is water: I understand it to be so in that it breaks down levels; it equalizes. Once anyone is inside music, there isn't a boss of it; the listener means as much as the players. And we aren't ourselves anymore, not quite, with our usual heaviness and dashed hopes. If anything, it makes us lighter, buoyant. We float.

Why would I do such a thing to myself, my spirit? People give up children. People leave beloved places behind for their families. People step out of their lives in middle age to care for an ailing parent. People put pleasures aside in order to become activists who help and save others. I gave up the one true thing I had that connected me to people. I'd been lonely as a child, and I'd brought myself closer to others through music, by playing with and for them. I saved my life through music. I gave it up.

~~~~~

Jude looked right into the camera as if he were looking into my face, even though to do so he had to be looking fully at himself, unafraid. With only two percussive notes on the piano, I knew he'd taught himself "Lesson in Survival" for me. And as I listened to his turns, holds, and spaces, I heard it as a brand-new thing: both *of* Joni and not. His playing wasn't so much about his ability to get it right, to *win* it, but to show me all the intricacies that lay inside what I thought I already knew, every detail that was too easy to miss, the song cracking open into a fresh field that wasn't simply *one thing* but an oncoming action of colors, stems, petals, and leaves, both browning and coming to life at once. See that violet, that yellow? Shepherd's needle, fire wheel, bog torch, buttonbush, chicory, cinnamon fern. *Maybe I'd never really loved,* and if I didn't crash into his arms like the speaker in "Amelia," I felt them around me, holding me in place. It was staggering to know that about myself after all this time, which only made me want to hold him harder, even though he wasn't in the room with me. And now it's just beginning? My life?

BOTH SIDES NOW

〜〜〜〜〜

IN 1967, A SEVEN-YEAR-OLD BOY IN CHERRY HILL, NEW JERSEY, sat before an upright piano, sounding individual keys. He'd walked by that piano a dozen times a day, but it had never occurred to him before to touch it. Maybe because it seemed too heavy, four times heavier than his own weight. Though his mother had recently painted it the color of a Spanish olive, it still conjured up solemnity, grief. It had been his grandmother's instrument, and the way his mother talked about it, his grandmother *was* the piano: she'd transferred into its hammers, wires, ivories, and keys the moment she'd fallen and broken her hip. He was afraid of his grandmother, but she was gone before he was old enough to remember her face. It was enough to know that she'd pounded on the instrument so hard after his uncle Paul's death that she'd worn the brass finish off the pedal with her shoe. Every time the boy looked down at the pedal, he saw it: a half-inch crescent-shaped gash. It always looked fresh, fresh enough to give off the fragrance of a penny handed from palm to palm. What kind of sorrow would make her pump the pedal like that? Maybe it was why his mother shied away from the piano, as if she'd already closed herself down, deciding she'd never had the depth to be a saint. For her it seemed preferable to behave as if the instrument were a graveyard between the kitchen and the foyer: the most traveled highway in the house.

When did I feel individual notes coalesce into a song? I couldn't tell if it happened all at once or over a matter of days, weeks. Every time I sat down on the bench, I stayed a while longer. It probably helped that it wasn't cordoned off in a separate room, away from the kitchen—otherwise, playing would have seemed precious, would have come with expectations from me, from others. It would have been too tempting to fail at it, to turn it into an assignment. The piano was out in the open, and it didn't matter if I played well or finished anything—more often than not, I played fragments—though I wanted my music to make my mother put her utensils down, walk over to me, kiss the back of my head, let her lips stay until they went dry. In a matter of time, I turned the instrument into a companion, an object as light as a guitar. I didn't want to do anything else but play, and if I did my homework or accompanied my father to the nursery, I couldn't wait to get home and be absorbed by it again. It was time to start including the sharps and flats, the low notes and the high. The center keys had already started to feel a bit too easy.

Somehow the hard work of it didn't feel like work. It didn't give me a headache, didn't make my stomach churn like so much else about being a solitary boy who had a hard time making friends, though I wanted them. I was making something only I could make. I felt important to myself, which was of a piece with sensing that my playing might make me important to others. What else did I have that would make someone else pay attention to me other than that I was sick all the time? Mononucleosis, mumps, chicken pox, German measles. Had Dr. Boguslaw mentioned cystic fibrosis? He was going to request some tests, and days later, even when they came back negative for that and other conditions, my mother treated me for the rest of my life as if I were endangered: a bluebird flown into a window. Yet this didn't stop her from being mad at me every time I told her my forehead felt hot. She lay her palm above my brows. *Again?* My head felt hotter. Her eyes filled with angst as if she now had to accommodate the ritual of possibly losing me again, which simultaneously managed to suppress my immune system, more out of worry for her than for myself.

She asked me questions from the kitchen, and I answered back, talking right over my playing. What was I playing? The folk songs I'd heard in church, bits of the pop songs I'd listened to on the radio or in the supermarket aisles. All I needed to do was to listen, absorb, and my brain recorded what I'd heard. Patterns of sound traveled to my fingers, the left hand approximating a bass line, though I didn't yet know that was what I was after. There'd be mistakes—I'm not saying there wasn't awkwardness or fumbling, but if I heard an A, I played an A. F? Same. Music was a picture or a sequence of images, a movie that didn't quite connect to itself, and it was just a matter of time before I was giving sound to the shapes.

Not once did my mother—or anyone—tell me to stop. Even back then I was thankful for that. They took for granted that I was the soundtrack of the house, but they never made a fuss over me or put any pressure on me the way they would to get all As in order to skip a grade or attend some gifted child program. My grades were already starting to slip. My playing was outside of that lust, which was always more about themselves than it was about me.

For my mother, my music might have sounded like the sonic equivalent of cooking, which she did on the other side of the half wall between us. It involved stops and starts, changing electric burners, shaking in some salt and pepper, maybe some olive oil, and didn't involve a preordained path.

"It's time for you to take lessons," she suggested one day.

"I have an idea," she said, though much later she'd insist that I'd begged for them. I went along with it if only because she sounded proud whenever she told the story to friends and relatives. It changed the sound of her voice, which went fuller, deeper.

~~~~~

I walked down a long sidewalk, stepped down the five steps past a concrete retaining wall stained bright green with moss. Inside the door: finished paneled basement. Four rows of empty folding chairs before a baby grand. Mr. Otterman waved me into Studio One with his usual grin, flyaway salt-and-pepper hair, mad scientist glasses low on his nose. As usual, we dispensed with sight-reading and scales and started playing, which involved making sure I didn't look down at my hands and kept my eyes up on the music rack. I was giving every note my attention, leaning in closer, moving my head from side to side—expressively. I was making it all up, with the exception of the melody. Did it bother me that after two months I didn't know the difference between a half and a quarter rest, a sixteenth note and an eighth? I was hoping that Mr. Otterman wouldn't notice if I played well enough, and when I reached the final chord, he cried, "That sounds better than the original." I half believed him, half sank in disappointment, as he'd already said these words seven times over the last eight weeks. Maybe he wasn't taking me seriously. Maybe he didn't take anyone very seriously, least of all himself, which accounted for the fact that I never showed up for lessons with cold hands or a groaning stomach. When I pulled out my assignment, a Top 40 song that I'd picked out in hopes that it would make me popular, he drew in closer to examine the lyrics my mother had crossed out for their suggestiveness. His lips moved in silence as he tried to make out words that seemed dirtier now for their half obliteration.

Sometimes I wondered why my parents hadn't taken me to study with Clement Petrillo, who lived around the corner from us, on Edgewood Drive. Clement Petrillo was one of the most respected piano teachers around, known for his classical rigor and feared for his punishing standards: he was the dean of the Philadelphia College of the Performing Arts. My mother believed that I was too sensitive to work with such a figure, but those thoughts seemed to have more to do with how she thought of herself. For her it was dangerous to aim too high. Aim too high and your wings of wax could melt into syrup. Aim too high and you could be humbled into a version of yourself that you couldn't possibly live with.

When Joni played her first composition for her piano teacher at seven, the teacher hit her across the knuckles with a ruler, the learning method in vogue: Why would you want to play by ear when you could have the masters at your fingers?

~~~~

It always came on me like a rogue wave on a calm sea. Not music, but as mysterious as music—and definitely connected to it. The desire that said, *I have to say it. I have to get it out, give it words, and someone—anyone—has to hear, and it doesn't even matter if they listen, but I hope they do.* Usually the news was ridiculous: The Thorns painted their front door blue. Or there's a bright red street sign on Middle Acre Lane. The terrible compulsion to share what I saw, and if I held it in, I'd drown in the sewer of it, smelly. Holding it in was like holding in pee, or holding my breath when an inner tube was around my waist, and the top half of me was pointing down to the bay bottom, and my legs were sticking up, kicking. My father, right beside me, thought I was making a joke. He didn't approve of jokes about such things—the boy who cried wolf a frequent example—and it didn't occur to him, even after he inverted me (choking, breathing, snot flying), how close I'd been to dying, an entire bay filling up my lungs with salt water.

～～～

In 1952, a nine-year-old girl in North Battleford, Saskatchewan, was walking home from Miss Fulford's fifth-grade class when a wave broke over her, ready to pull her under. Headache, tiredness, neck and back stiff. Euphoria? She thought she was going to throw up. "Oh dear," she said, "I'm getting old. I must have rheumatism, 'cause my grandmother had rheumatism." The day before, she'd looked into a mirror and thought, *You look like a woman today.* Her face had redistributed itself, more leanness, less fat. The circles underneath her eyes unsettled her, and the child she'd been was no longer reachable. *Goodbye, child.* She was an adult now.

She sat down on the curb, unable to go forward in her pegged gray slacks, the red-and-white gingham blouse she'd picked out herself. She pulled the back of her blue sweater around her shoulders for warmth, but still she heard her teeth chattering.

In hours she was airlifted to St. Paul's Hospital in Saskatoon, the polio clinic. Flying engines. The drone of them. If only she could move, look out the window, and see her house down there. The church where she sang in the upstairs choir, the movie theater. Little checkerboard town all by itself in a sea of wheat.

The next day there was an empty desk in the classroom, an empty chair pushed under the desk. Did the room feel different without her? Did it register her absence? Would everyone pretend the light was still the same through the windows? The person who drew well—did anyone miss her pictures of forests and animals? Or was she just a number as the room grew larger and the people in it dwindled? Another soldier down.

She shared the room at the polio clinic with a little boy. The air was sour, suffocating, and to pass the hours, he and Joni watched the snow falling against the windowpane. Snow was beautiful, but it kept everyone inside and turned instantly to water as soon as it touched hot glass. Winter, which lurked all year, even on a cold morning in the midst of summer.

She lay flat on her back as directed—she didn't want to end up in one of those big cans. *Lungs*, they called them, as if its job wasn't to make you a part of a machine. Stiffness, stillness. Clock on the wall, tissues. Drinking glass stained with orange juice. When would she walk again? If she couldn't walk again, how could she leave her parents' house? How could she watch birds and deer, put her hands down in the earth when it thawed in April? How could she lie down in the leaves, look up, and let the sky in?

~~~~~

Parents weren't encouraged to visit, and so they left her alone, except the one time her mother came by with a Christmas tree with lights strung on its boughs. Her mother wore a mask, her eyes haunted, already attempting to take in what she believed to be inevitable. After she left, the girl didn't pray to God but prayed to the angel at the top of the tree. "If I could get my legs back . . ." She prayed so hard. Prayed against her doctor, a polio survivor who used a wheelchair, who told her she wouldn't be able to return home for the holidays. Prayed against the nurses, who should have smiled more. And so she submitted to the scalding rags and gave in to the therapist's request to bend her stiff body. She sang Christmas carols at the top of her lungs and didn't care when anybody flinched, turned their heads away from her shrieking.

If I'd been sixteen years older and grown up not in New Jersey but in Canada, I might have been the little boy who shared the room with her. I might have been afraid. I might not have known what to do with all her fury and will, her disinterest in being nice in all the socially expected ways. But I wasn't so interested in people who were conventionally nice. I was drawn to the effort of having to win over such a person, and people like that always loved me more for it, treated me as if I were special. Maybe if I kept quiet, maybe if I listened to her, she'd talk even more, and I'd have someone to watch and listen to—better than all the movies I was missing, all locked up in a hot room. Maybe when she felt better, she'd give me orders. This clown, this page. Take that yellow crayon and color in his hat. Put a pom-pom on that hat.

And when I handed it back to her, she wouldn't have looked at it strangely, disparagingly. She would have nodded and offered encouragement. *Don't be afraid to press harder. The pom-pom deserves color. Wouldn't you want color on you if you were a pom-pom?*

When all was said and done, her spine "looked like a freeway after an earthquake," as she told Cameron Crowe in *Rolling Stone*. It got her right leg too.

Five years later she'd go out dancing with her friends on weekends. None of them would have guessed that she'd come so close to being paralyzed, that she hadn't always been some good-time Charlie.

~~~~~

For chorus we stood in four neat rows. It was a relief to be neat after the chaos of the playground, where someone was always ready to come up from behind and punch you, make you look stupid, no matter your response, whether you looked hurt or ashamed, or ignored it. These horrors weren't the same horrors of my previous school, a Catholic school, where a lay teacher had the principal's okay to hit you if you talked back, or embarrass you if you hid between the wet coats of the cloakroom.

I was a tall boy, which meant I was in the back row. I didn't yet know that I was tall. I'd just assumed everyone else could see over the heads of their classmates. I didn't know what others seemed to know: that I had an advantage and could get special favors for it. In my innocence, I experienced my height as a liability. It made me stand out when I didn't want anyone to lay their eyes on me, make fun of me.

If I did have to stand out, I wanted it to be for something I did well, a project that required practice and dedication, a skill no one else could do. I wanted to do it so well that people couldn't help but love me and say, *We were wrong about you; will you forgive us? All that talk about your ears sticking out too far from the sides of your head, your complete ignorance about games and their rules. What were we thinking? How can we make it up to you?*

In return, no one would train their floodlights on me again. They wouldn't categorize and rank me according to how I fit inside some outline. Clumsiness, the wrong walk or vocal pitch. *Sissy:* vicious sting out of nowhere. Instead, they'd look at me as if all those qualities were part of my special gifts, and they'd decide to love me all the more for them. But I knew none of that came without work, in spite of my ability to play by ear. I had to be front and center on the stage, offered up like USDA Choice beef for inspection. I had to risk embarrassment and failure and show others I could win the song I set out to play. And if I had to try four times harder than other people?

Love didn't come without tests. Anything of worth demanded a test.

~~~~~

Mrs. Hill pushed the upright piano through the fourth-grade classroom door, a feat she accomplished once a week, every Tuesday, in the hour before school let out. There was a mightiness about her, which I might have missed if she weren't so short and her blond hair weren't so high, pretzeled on top of her head. Her miniskirt came up higher than it should have, and she pulled it downward as she talked to us, as if its crawl were merely bothersome, even natural. No one shared mocking expressions behind her back as they did when other guests came to visit the class. Maybe because she was bringing music, and music calmed us. It was a gift; it dissolved rivalry, a chocolate cake she'd carried into the room and cut into twenty pieces. Mrs. Hill made music feel like it was meant for everyone, not just those with special talents, even if she appreciated those with talent—she didn't play her favorites against anyone. Thus people who didn't have the remotest concept of pitch yelled out the songs she taught us as if they were getting to know their lungs, lips, and breathing for the first time. I could live with their enthusiasm if it turned the whole group of us toward a good mood.

Usually Mrs. Hill picked songs in which children were supposed to sound like children. The songs were often about weather and generally upbeat—"Windy," "Raindrops Keep Fallin' on My Head," "Let the Sunshine In"—which was another way to say that children were supposed to be happy. If the children weren't happy, then what did that say about their teachers and parents? Perhaps it suggested that they hadn't done a very good job, that they'd screwed up something that was too far gone to fix, and so it was up to the children to make sure the adults in charge felt successful in every way they knew. We'd show them that they'd taken good care of us.

But today's song was different. It sounded happy on first listen, but on closer inspection, heartbroken at the same time. The person who had written it had lost things, I felt that, but the source of that sadness was deeper than merely growing up, changing, leaving a house and hometown behind. Maybe it was just that angel hair and ice cream castles were trying so hard to say that lightness lived alongside darkness. When I sang the song, my face grew long. The skin above my upper lip felt weighted.

I hadn't known that I'd missed that feeling until I realized it was something to miss.

And when I came home, I played the song by ear until it sounded like I'd always known it, and I couldn't hear all the erasures and repetitions that went into its making.

~~~~

Joni sat by the plane window, looking out at the clouds. Saul Bellow's novel *Henderson the Rain King* lay open on her tray table, but she kept orbiting the same paragraph, because she was more interested in the clouds outside in all their layers and dimensions, the range of colors from slate to fog to purest white. How could they be described? Muscular, Michelangelo—she thought of naked Adam touching God's outstretched finger. Maybe she'd already gotten what she'd wanted from the book—the picture of the narrator, Henderson, looking at a similar view on a flight to Africa—and to read beyond that would obscure what she wanted her heart and mind to hold. Henderson's insight? He was living during the first time in history when humans could look at clouds from above and below. Sometimes a book said all it needed to say in a picture. Sometimes a song did as well.

Clouds called to her. If she looked at them long enough, she could pull them up inside her and get to know them. She could *become* clouds if she tried hard enough. She could conjure them up on her guitar until the chords she played sounded wet. She'd have to dry off the rain from her hands.

The new song came together quickly, and she was performing it on Gene Shay's radio show in Philadelphia when it was only a couple days old. She felt proud of the song as she played and sang it, but she didn't seem to know that it stood out from any of her other songs. Surely it was more straightforward, without the complex chords and melodic leaps, qualities that her fellow musicians thought of with simultaneous envy and dismissal as Joni moved. A lot of people could have written this song—at least its melody and chords. She was writing all the time, the archive was growing every day, and she didn't have to worry so much about whether one song was better than the other, because a new one might emerge as she was testing the pegs for a new tuning.

She wouldn't know that Judy Collins would soon call her up in the middle of the night, asking to record what would turn out to reach number eight on the US singles chart. Wouldn't know that 1,616 other singers would record the song: Frank Sinatra, Harry Belafonte, Bing Crosby, Glen Campbell—the kinds of musicians her parents would listen to on their living room record player. Wouldn't know that, decades later, it would be central to at least two movies, one of which would win the Academy Award for Best Picture. Had she stopped there, a whole career could have thrived on that foundation. When she went backstage to congratulate Mabel Mercer for her performance of the song, Joni told her that it needed the voice of an older woman, someone with life experience. "And what do *you* know about suffering?" Mabel said in plummy disapproval. Joni hadn't mentioned that she was the writer of the song. Of course she'd known plenty about suffering through polio, through teaching herself how to walk a second time, but perhaps she took some satisfaction that she could pass as unharmed.

Pain wasn't always written on her face.

~~~~~

Danger was rarely what they told you it was. Not the ice on the lake, wet and sloppy from the sunshine. Not the poison at the bottom of the iodine bottle with the skull and crossbones on the label. Not the plane flying too low over the roof, veering toward the vents in the chimney that held a sparrow's nest with eggs inside.

No, when it appeared, it was often as personal as a face. Someone who was supposed to be looking out for you. They believed they were doing exactly that, then all at once, started testing you, deciding that you were the enemy, pushing you away without giving you any explanation as to why. Maybe it was just that the two of you felt too close, and someone needed to hurt someone else to keep the line between you intact.

It could have been your mother when she'd had enough of you.

Other times it was none other than yourself, or yourself anticipating that critical person so you could get there first, avert the disaster. The words ran together, the voice practically simultaneous. It said, *You can't do it, nothing in you can change the way things are, you don't have what it takes, you aren't good, you don't have what it takes, you aren't good, you don't have the discipline, the persistence, you're a quitter, why are you always the last person to see that you're a quitter?*

And every note struck on the keyboard was a no. Every vowel out of your mouth. It was even a no just to pull the bench back from the piano with the intention to play. It kept your back straight, steeled for the punch, should it ever come from some stranger—or even a friend—behind you.

~~~~~

Mrs. Hill pushed the piano out through the classroom door, a feat no less impressive after the physical work of all that singing and waving her arms around. My classmates had already left the building, running out onto the blacktop to get on their buses. There wasn't much time, as I had some rubber steps to climb up too. I heard the words before I spoke them. They broke through the surface, cresting around a shoal. I'd never asked anyone for a favor before, especially an adult who wasn't my father or mother. She looked at me through her glasses, looked straight into my eyes, as if whatever I had to say was practical, news she'd been waiting to hear from me. These were not the days when parents thought people of my age then were important. They left us alone. They let us roam away from our backyards, where we could be gone for hours, collecting stones, pushing tadpoles around, setting fires to piles of broken sticks and running away. There was freedom in this model, but adults and children didn't have a clue as to how to talk to one another. The divide was too wide.

What did I ask? It was as simple as asking if I could play the piano—solo—for the next school concert.

I don't know how I did it without turning my head away or letting my eyes fall in shame.

Goodbye, child. I was an adult now.

An exhaustion came over me, as if I were a fish, and a net had been dropped from above, and inside I was thrashing but silent and moving my mouth. I felt as if I were asking more from life than I deserved, and what if she said, *Are you kidding? You're putting me in an awful position. You want too much—why you and not Todd Magnat or Eve Murakami?*

You're very talented, but they're talented too, Paul.

I hadn't come up with a backup plan, and the thought of that almost made me topple over.

"Play for me," she said, calmly. She took a step backward, hugging herself. A cold draft blew from the vent in the ceiling above.

My broken heart, I thought, but without the words.

"Keep going," she said after I looked over my shoulder. "I'm here."

And that was exactly what I did for her.

~~~~~

One day I found the woman whose songs I liked in the bin at the Korvette's record department. By then I knew her name was Joni Mitchell and had imagined what she looked like, but it was still a shock to see her face, not in one of my dreams but in public, where people bought bath towels, irons, nail polish, and St. Joseph Aspirin for Children. The album featured a self-portrait against a backdrop of woods; a river; some low clouds; layers of yellow, orange, ochre, claret. A red lily held up to her face. A face as wide open as a mountain lion's, eyes as clear as water in a stream. It wanted to assure you that calm was possible, but maybe in order to get to that calm, you had to suffer first. In the background, a castle: Bavarian with high roof peaks. Later I'd find out that it was the Bessborough Hotel, a railway-era landmark in Saskatoon, where Joni encamped whenever she went back to visit her hometown. But I thought of it as a hospital then. Low lights humming in the windows. Both sunrise and sunset in that sky at once. As much darkness as illumination. That darkness easy to miss at first. The cover was a lot like the song. It drew you in with its optimism before showing you that turbulence was a given. Turbulence was the engine that made the trees grow behind her.

If I looked long enough at that face, I would feel the space growing between the two of us. I turned away for a second. No one would have ever mistaken us for relatives, not even distant.

~~~~~

In another time, in a different body, I would have walked up to the stage, and the people would have clapped before I sat down to play the piano. I'd nod, both appreciative and patient. Maybe I'd even give them a smile, so broad it was on the edge of plastic, before waiting for everyone to settle down. Once I'd begin to play, the whole room would go silent, no one shifting in their chairs, no one yawning or stepping around people's legs and bags for a bathroom break or a smoke outside by the flagpole. I would have felt calmed by that silence, not afraid of it, as if it were a sign that I'd made everyone feel a little more alive in a world that wanted to dull us at every turn, that wanted to take our shine away. And what did that make us do? It made a lot of us mean when we didn't want to be mean. People wanted to be better than that. That was their secret.

Instead, something else happened.

I was playing the third verse, and the floor holding up the

room opened. The sounds that I had been taking for granted beneath my fingers went strange, and the grid that had been holding us all together collapsed. No, not collapsed, nothing as extreme as all that. Instead, the squares of the grid went loose, as if they'd grown tired of holding something inside. I felt how strange it was to be a nine-year-old boy, with arms, legs, and fingers, and an occasionally mangled last name, in this school auditorium in New Jersey, which probably wouldn't be around in a hundred years or even less. The people out in those chairs wouldn't be around in a hundred years, not a single one of them, and I felt terrible for them, for all the life they'd miss, the birthdays, the music, the days at the beach or in the woods. Buying things: shoes, groceries. I felt that they couldn't handle that about themselves. And what carried me, or the people in those chairs, was a different set of notes—I'd wandered away from the notes I'd been playing. Did anyone notice or care? If they did, they didn't betray it on their faces, no frowns or looks of concern, not even from Mrs. Hill, who stood backstage, behind the curtain patterned with cherries, looking at me with the face of love, a love that was different from the love that came from my parents. She wanted the best for me. I knew that my version was good, which is not to say that I thought I was improving the song. I was turning it toward a direction that sounded like me, to how my hands wanted to reach, curl, and contract. It was all of three measures, ten seconds. The time was 8:10. The clock on the wall told me so. Then the grid reinforced itself, and I was back to the world of rules, routines, punishments, and expectations. It sent me forth into the crowd to sit down between my parents.

LESSON IN SURVIVAL

THE PEOPLE STREAMED INTO CARNEGIE HALL FROM WEST Fifty-Seventh Street, trying not to push. They anxiously compared the numbers and letters on their tickets. Would the person in front of them have a giant head or babble throughout the concert? Would someone in the next seat scream, *I love you, Joni,* during the most tender parts of "I Had A King"? Everyone was well-behaved, which didn't mean they didn't have the capacity to kill for what they believed in. Her singing was always meant to be one on one. She was there to say, *I know what you feel. I'm singing* yourself *for you, but I'm going to trick you into thinking it's all about me, so you don't have to feel exposed.* Changing the equation of that was like conducting psychoanalysis in a public forum. They wanted her to themselves, and could anyone be blamed? That's why they were there. It was a testament to human behavior that people weren't already arguing and tearing into one another's skin fifteen minutes before the houselights went down. It was February 1, 1969. In about six months a man would stand on the moon, and less than a month later, Woodstock. By the end of the year, a concertgoer would be murdered at Altamont, and any ideas about the Summer of Love would seem as quaint as Joni's singing before she ever stepped foot in a recording studio.

Joni's mother and father were there for her first big concert. Joni wore a skirt with a sequined American eagle on the front and an artichoke on the back, while Graham Nash, her boyfriend, was head to toe in black velvet, pink-and-white tie-dyed scarf at his throat. They were rushing from the Plaza Hotel to the concert hall, running a little late. Though they passed all kinds of people in every situation imaginable, Joni's mother couldn't get over how absurd the two of them looked. What was this, a costume party? Why these rags? It was hard for her not to bring up those outfits backstage, and when she could no longer hold it back, it wasn't appreciated, but someone had to say it. She knew that she was saving her daughter from looking ridiculous on the Carnegie Hall stage. If your own mother couldn't say it, then who could? She clasped the latch on her handbag.

Myrtle and Bill sat in the audience, in the front row. The people beside them seemed a little fidgety and dumb to Myrtle, but then again, everyone she'd met on this trip felt a little dumb, as polite as they tried to be. Maybe there was no escaping this side of people when they found out she was Joni's mother. They became not only obsequious but something more disconcerting, as if they walked away from themselves. They wanted things from her, a little piece of Joni's past, a funny story, her recipe for pork chops, all of which she found distasteful. She could have told them about the poodle-shaped record box, her five-pin bowling trophies, but if she had, they'd only want more. No surprise given the dirty laundry hung out to dry in her daughter's songs.

The hall went dark. Screams, which went on way too long, made her want to cover her ears, but she would have looked like a monster, so she sat with her head high and her back as straight as possible. She tapped Bill above the knee, startling him, without knowing exactly why she did it, what she was asking of him, though maybe she needed to feel him as separate when all she wanted to do was to coalesce into him, the big, dull care of him, his trumpet-playing past. There was her daughter, looking not like her daughter but some impostor, up on the stage, so high up there, it made Myrtle's neck hurt to take her all in. With breasts. With that ridiculous artichoke sewn over her precious rear end—rags! She did half roll her eyes, and then closed them so anyone looking at her would think it was a twitch.

People were looking at her, scanning her for reaction. There was no way to get out from under their scrutiny.

To watch your only daughter be adored by so many people. To see their hunger, to hear it, to smell how it altered their sweat, made their clothes give off a musk. There was too much feeling in the air, and she was suspicious of feeling, always had been, from the time she felt the urge to leave Saskatchewan and never come back. To go there would have been a call to dismantle her life. What right did a daughter have to dismantle her mother's life? All the things she'd done to bring her daughter to this place—where else did Joni's appreciation for color, meticulousness, order, come from if not from all of her lessons and examples? Her love of words, plants, and animals; her poise; her grace? But Joni wouldn't see that, no. She chose to align herself with the crass young people of her generation who chose to resent their parents, who would walk around a Greek island with bare, muddy feet, crude oil and grime encrusting their toenails. It felt like everything Myrtle had given her—the lessons on style, the care, the clothes, the permission to paint a black tree covering her bedroom wall—had been turned inside out, made darker and stranger until it felt like it was all part of a dirty joke that wouldn't stop.

Her daughter was laughing at her, taking potshots at her, but in song.

The night was out of Myrtle's control. And the idiom Joan used in her songs—*ain't, don't. Wrong.* That wasn't how Joan talked, at least not around her. It wasn't how the daughter of a schoolteacher talked. Phony, pretentious: it was as if Joan were contorting herself to be a country person, from Kentucky or North Carolina. And the applause between songs? It was just swelling a head that was already big enough, thank you. If she'd used words like that back in Saskatoon, they would have laughed her off Broadway Avenue. And as Myrtle thought these things, she imagined Joan looking down at her face, midfrown. Everything she'd never wanted her daughter to see was on display, and she blushed all the way to her roots, as if someone had taken a match to her.

And maybe that was when she heard the music for the first time. Maybe that was when she felt something touch her in an uncomfortable place, a private place, where she hadn't been touched in a long time. It scared her—a little. The touch both soothed and scraped, because in that moment, Joan was no longer *of* her but her own creature, separate. Myrtle felt an inkling that she'd never felt before: they were both going to die. And in that moment, she had to say goodbye not just to herself but to Joan. And there was nothing she could do to protect her, like there was nothing she'd been able to do to stop her daughter's muscles from stiffening up, which meant going away to that awful clinic that she'd hated driving to but not as much as she'd hated leaving. Looking at her up there when she could have been dead, and she'd already prepared herself for the possibility. There wasn't another child in her life, and there never would be, no one as exquisite. As for herself? She was smaller in every way: spirit, talent, vivacity, brilliance. Everyone else in this hall knew that she was sitting in front of a messenger, some visitor from another realm, and she was the last one to figure it out. And there she was, naked to herself: someone who had never known enough about music, someone who didn't have the persistence it required, someone who was no longer young but dressed and behaved like someone from Saskatchewan, drilled to be modest, trained to conceal excessive emotion. The music slumped over her like netting, lifting her. She'd been thinking of herself as outside of the room, away from New York City, but that was too easy, that wasn't helping, and when she looked up at the building, the boat of it, the tiers, the railings, the domes—all she felt was alone. Her beautiful daughter. And no music, even if it made the girl behind her cry, was going to bring the two of them closer.

~~~~

Nine years had passed since my earliest days at the piano.

It wasn't something I'd planned, but it wasn't just something that simply happened to me either. A little bit of both, this writing of songs. I knew if I'd made a big deal of it in my mind, I would have delayed it, been cautious of it. Instead, I approached it the way I approached learning the piano. Thoughts of accomplishment and recognition simply fell away, my eyes focusing on the keys. I had a spiral-bound notebook of music staff paper. I darkened its pages with open black ovals, two-tiered flags, indecipherable rests, sometimes two songs to a page. Five songs a week, maybe more. I stopped counting after a couple weeks.

The songs were as much drawings as they were songs. By that I mean I turned them into pictures just as they were coming into being. I needed to anchor them before they could slide away and disappear. The songs looked serious on the staves, even if my quarter notes were too thick and filled more space than was required. My notebook gave the songs a legitimacy. They made it look like I knew what I was doing, even if I was, for a little while, keeping the songs to myself, a melodic version of a diary.

But maybe I should have let the songs wander and shape-shift before I set them down. Often I thought I should have let them live in the air or in the cabinet of my imagination before I wrestled them, fixed them. Joni didn't read music. Joni seemed to distrust everything about the conventional mapping of music, and that wasn't laziness. She couldn't have written the songs she'd written if she hadn't made up her own language, if she'd been fixated on middle C, and the key of F, and the root of the chord. But I was too timid not to learn the rules. Maybe because so many of life's rules seemed far away from me, took concentration. If I didn't at least get to know them, I'd spin off and be incomprehensible to others. I already felt too much like a weirdo. Joni could get away with being a weirdo in her music because she exuded charm and appeared to be friendly and unthreatening, someone you wouldn't be afraid to sit down with. Even if you were that awkward freak in the cafeteria, she'd come over to you and ask how you were doing, pour some of her chocolate milk into your empty glass.

When I looked at my work on the page, all the life was in the chords. I'd made a meadow of growth, from page to page, but my meadow needed space and light. *Melody. Shape.* It wasn't simply enough to stack up chord changes as if the voice didn't really matter. My own voice sounded like soil when I wanted it to sound like sky, cold and clear. I couldn't lift it up to that register, so my songs stayed down in the soil for a while, among the roots, earthworms, petrichor.

~~~~~

There was no way you could make anything without confronting what didn't work about it. Making art of any sort was about learning to sit next to failure; if not exactly holding its hand, then riding in the back seat with it, listening to it going on and on about its plans to be *The Toast of New York City* when you just wanted to tell it to shut up and say something of genuine interest. Or maybe you had to start to learn to love the failure as if he were your child. You didn't stop loving him because he turned out to be a football player when you really wanted him to be a painter—he was so good at painting. You asked him what you were missing, what you weren't seeing in his wish to grip the ball by its stitches, his desire to be a part of a team. And he'd nod to the gravel at the edge of the patio as if he could see that there would always be distance between you, a distance that couldn't be bridged. He knew that he wasn't you, and he was already better at handling that problem.

~~~~

If I'd started writing songs for an audience, it wouldn't have been long before I had to write the expected kind of song, a love song. Love is religion for most people. It isn't invisible, remote, high up in the sky. To them, it isn't a phantom just out of reach, its form ever changing but in bodies they can see, kiss, touch, and try to get inside of.

But love was something that happened to others. It wasn't intended for someone like me. The person I had in mind—I wasn't allowed to walk down the school hall with him without being called names, beaten up, maybe worse. No one else I knew risked that. So how would I have written a love song without risking false notes? Copying other people's ideas of love when I wasn't even allowed to be interested in love, as likely as digging a hole where I stood and finding flecks of gold?

And even if I did fall in love or had a crush—could I write such a song? If I wrote it, I'd have to turn the object of my love into a girl or a woman, and wouldn't everybody see through me? There had to be ways to get around this problem, smart ways, but they weren't coming to me. This wasn't an era in which men sang love songs to other men. They would soon enough—The Smiths—but not yet. The examples I heard on the University of Pennsylvania's WXPN made me uncomfortable, sometimes cringe, as well-intentioned as they were. Maybe it was that the love in those songs had to be purer than the love in the songs of straight people. Love without impediment and obstacle. Love without argument. Gay love was perfect love, and politics wanted those songs to be as positive and uplifting as the songs of Doris Day. My father's crush, long after her heyday.

So I started setting the texts and responsorial psalms I'd heard in church. It was easier to write about God or, more precisely, God's love for his people than human-to-human love, which was always about sex, though it pretended not to be. God's love seemed comprehensible—or at least steady—in the passages we heard in church. God was a known commodity. God was clean; God had sharper borders than romance, which was always on the threshold of turning against itself. It seemed to need that threshold in order to be romance. But to set psalms to music felt like I was cheating or I'd given up somehow. Settling for what was right there, already well described, in front of me. Even if hardly anyone believed in God anymore.

How could you believe in such a worldview when you had astronauts gyrating in a tin can above you?

The people who sat in the hard black chairs of my church— did they believe in God? Did they believe enough to struggle and doubt—could they be angry with God? Or did they come back to mass every Sunday because it was just another marker in the schedule, another check mark on the calendar? The thing they did before they went out to Olga's Diner, where everybody at the booth ordered waffles, whether they liked to eat waffles or not, because it was tradition.

When two people love each other, they can't help but hurt, or be wounded, or die from longing—that was what I gleaned from songs and movies, and definitely what I saw between my parents. And the more they loved each other, the stronger the capacity for sorrow and breakage and confusion grew. And maybe that was why the landscape of the psalms felt comfortable to me. The worst God did to you, me, the lady across the street? He didn't show His face when you needed Him. He kept himself busy with helping others. But it wasn't like He wasn't always keeping an eye out for you too. He didn't tell you that He loved you at dinner. He didn't touch your face and drive away, leaving you stranded at a romantic restaurant while others looked on, pretending not to see how you were doing, whether you were shredding the napkin in your hand or your eyes were misting up. And when you picked up the phone, God wasn't looking into someone else's eyes, His ankle hooked around another's. He was saying, *Hey, Paul, I believe in you.*

If I were practical, if I'd had some sense of limit, I would've listened to some Top 40 songs and seen what I could learn from their structure and constraints. I'd have been satisfied with one surprising chord in the hinge from verse to hook. I'd have given some thought as to why they were meaningful to people across categories, across generations. But sense was not my specialty. Instead, I listened to Joni's *For the Roses*, humbled, dazzled, shocked by its ingenuity on every listen. But the truth? It never intimidated me. I didn't have the audacity to think I could write songs like that, but I had enough audacity to think I could approximate some of her chords in standard tuning. This was a virtue of being young, untested. I could sharpen my words; I could make them picturesque, not loading them up with adjectives but keeping them clean with images. I knew there was so much I couldn't yet see and hear about her songs, and that's what I loved about them.

On *For the Roses*, Joni's piano parts sounded like chamber music, but as if the nineteenth century were being reinterpreted freshly in the late twentieth, with staggered rhythms, unexpected notes in the root, and dissonance. The harmonies weren't chained to old patterns, and until I listened closely, I didn't realize how many old patterns held music, or at least popular music, in place. But was this pop music? It wanted to pass as such, but it was never so simple. It was too meticulous to be understood in one sitting, even six. Instead it was some conglomeration of folk, pop, country, and jazz, the spaces too close to pull them apart.

It wasn't just the songs that caught me but her voice too. It sounded like honey had been poured onto it—or perhaps California had been: its colors, brightness, smog, lavender, weeds, piers, palms, side streets, surface streets. Freeways! Laurel Canyon, Lookout Mountain Avenue. The Golden West. Not a simple California but one that had an ache in it. It was a voice that knew there was the deepest loneliness inside those houses, serrated leaves covering dark windows.

Maybe that was it—the music of loneliness. Loneliness didn't always sound like I expected it to sound. It was layered with happiness and hope. It could be joyful and connected to people and still be loneliness. Once you shut the door, it was just you inside, staring at the square of light holding its shape on the wall. Quivering, like water in a glass during seismic activity.

Standard tuning kept the strings in balance. It kept the sound tight, orderly, reliable. Once you twisted the tuning knobs to alternate pitches, the strings went slack, especially the lowest and the thickest. They buzzed when struck, while the tops strings relaxed. All six strings balanced on the brink of veering out of tune, and that made for a messiness, which was beautiful, otherworldly, if you loved loose ends, the sound of an experience that wasn't overly *finished*. Sometimes the chords sounded like they were pinned high on the fretboard, near the body. Sometimes the strings weren't fingered at all, open and loose, in the manner of a raga. In such instances, Joni could strum the instrument while lifting her left hand off the neck for a measure or two, and it still sounded phenomenal, depending on the tuning she used. I didn't know how to name a single one of her chords because the tunings challenged the standard musical language, all the rules I'd taken in through osmosis. They frustrated all the old ways I was able to transfer what I'd heard and bring them to the keyboard. A C major chord was easy to replicate. A C major 7 was too, but a C major 7/F? *That* overwhelmed my brain with the unexpected note outside the triad, at the root. My cortex didn't know what to do with an equation like that, but that didn't stop me from trying to get it down.

She'd cracked open the staff and found new notes in it. Well, maybe those notes were already there, but no one else had the imagination and drive to find them.

I couldn't listen to her work without putting everything else aside. Its scrupulousness demanded complete attention, and to give anything less than that would be to cheat myself, cheat music. Why would you not want to take full advantage?

When I listened to "See You Sometime," it gave me the sense that only I appreciated it, only I could hear that phrase, that note, that level and layer. Why? The song called on me to give it my full attention, to put everything else aside to listen or else I'd miss some chordal movement, some unexpected bass note, the reference to the apple orchard in too much rain. Its artistry believed that the song mattered, that my time mattered. It believed in *me*, in the possibility of my conjuring up not just the playful longing in the song but the Sunshine Coast landscape that inspired it: the kelp at the bottom of the Salish Sea. The octopus hiding between rocks, purpled, a little shy.

~~~

On the album cover, Joni dressed in forest-green velour, both shirt and pants, and tan suede boots. She was sitting on a rock with her knee up, green water and arbutus behind her. Her hair was straight, blond, maybe recently wet. There were bangs, strands falling to her shoulders in layers. She looked intelligent and curious. She wasn't making any claims: *I am suffering, I am desiring, I am beautiful, I am at peace.* Nor was she implying, *I am a person of the woods—you should be too. You should be macrobiotic, vegan, do yoga, try Reiki*—no. She was somewhere between a woman and a man, between old and young, a nature person and a city person. She wasn't torn between these opposites, not that. She held these opposites together as she'd always done. Busy being free. Both sides now.

The cover was blue-green, which poured into every song, even when the songs weren't near water. It was always an album in water, of water. The sea and the woods and where they touched each other.

Inside the cover, she turned her back to us. She was standing on a rock, naked. *Naked.* No sense that she was showing off or trying to be sexy. She was simply saying, *I'm a part of this—this rock, this ocean, this sky, these waves and green water.*

What other singer would be naked inside an album that came out in 1972? Who else would have shown us, so casually, her ass?

When my friend Holly looked at this picture, she said with casual confidence that Joni had a bad body. I didn't understand women's bodies—or feel them—enough to know what a bad body was. She didn't say it with meanness; she didn't go on and on about it. Still, it hurt me, as if she were talking of my own body, what I couldn't discern about it. What errors was she seeing that I couldn't see? Her posture, the width of her hips, her shoulders, the hint of a slouch? Or did Holly defile this body because it held such reverence to me, and it was unsettling to behold reverence in anyone, especially in a world that was hungry to tear down, make fun, roll eyes, even when the people who did it were otherwise decent? They were just recycling what they thought was expected of them. It was what happened when money and rating were the primary values.

But this was a picture of awe. It was always intended more for Joni than it was for us, and maybe the best art comes from that place, which isn't the same thing as saying it is selfish.

The wonder of being on one's feet without help. Imagine it. Her body was never the same after she had to teach herself how to walk a second time.

~~~~~

Inside, another drawing in felt pen, magenta, pink, green, brown, gold. A face. It looked ecstatic, that face. It took in the sweet smell of the roses. There were no eyes in that face—or just barely. Emotion erased all defining features. The edge of a chin obscured by roses. What did this drawing have to do with the photograph? Why were they so close to each other that my mind misremembered them as if they were two images, side by side?

Two sides of the performer: one private, one public. This one public. The singer, in gratitude, expressing her appreciation. Was she loving those flowers, emblem of the audience's love, too much? Was something dangerous being captured here: worship as a drug? What happened when the crowd grew tired of the performer, moving on to the next? What happened when the record company balked at low sales and used that as a condition to start controlling everything from how to what you sang? The clothes you wore, your shoes. The words that came out of your mouth when it was time to talk about yourself in interviews. Even when someone was disrespectful to you, which happened more frequently than not.

I went back and forth between the two images, looking for a conversation. The picture on the rocks? Joni turning her back on us. Human approval didn't matter to her, at least in this moment of forgetfulness and peace. If there was anything meaningful, it was out there in the water, beyond the waves. In what no human being could see, even Joni.

~~~~~

There wasn't a song that didn't leave its bruise beneath my skin. "Banquet," the opening. A song built on a list of contrasts, a catalogue. The greedy, the needy. The images were so rich, I could practically touch them as I listened. And yet in spite of all its

everyday glory, a bright day along the Sunshine Coast, the world
it evoked was ruined by the junk on the tide, the suggestion being
that humans couldn't interact with the beautiful without ruining
it, rubbing their scent on it. I would have loved its music if it came
without words, but its words cut into me. They made little movies
that flashed and dissolved before another took its place. The stream
kept flowing—for a little while. And in the wake of these songs,
so many other songs sounded lazy, too satisfied with themselves,
not interested in reaching for their potential complexities. They
borrowed. They sounded like more of the same but got away with
making you think they were new, even though they were simply
putting a spin on the familiar. Mediocrity was their drug of choice,
their smoke. They weren't nearly as interested in waking you up,
keeping you nervous and alive, as if lyrics were always intended to
be placeholders, just a means to give the singer something round
to hold on to.

~~~~~

The box lay wrapped in sleek white paper, an approximation of
staff paper, on my bed, near the pillows. It took a minute to make
out what it was. There was no reason to get a present now, as
my birthday was in July, but my mother intuited I needed some
cheering up—as every teenager needs cheering up—but it was not
something I'd wanted anyone to see written on my face. It was just
like her to buy me something when I was feeling down. I wanted
to say, *Don't. Please don't, because if you give me a reward for feeling
sad, I'm going to stay down there. You're training me to be that person
because that's the only kind of person you know. If you break me, I'll*

stay close to you, take care of you. I'd rather you buy me a present when there's a genuine reason to celebrate.

The space between us, already wide those days, stayed wide.

I pulled off the paper, first with caution, then ripped it away as if we'd never been the kind of family that stored sheets of used wrapping paper at the back of the closet to reuse. The box beneath it was printed with the logo of Strawbridge & Clothier, the department store where my mom worked when she was young. I was clearly going to find a shirt, but it wasn't anything bought at a store, no. Forest-green velour. I held it up to myself, beneath my chin. It was long the way my body was long. My mother? She'd made this, made it on her sewing machine when I was away at school. And the only way she could have done it was to hunt for the album in my stack, study Joni's outfit, and draw up a pattern.

Inside the collar she'd stitched a custom-made label with her name printed in signature form: *Fashioned by Anne H. Lisicky.*

Her art.

I held it up to my nose, breathed. It smelled of formaldehyde, as if it hadn't been washed yet, as if it were too precious to wash. I stopped up my sounds with the collar. I didn't want her out in the kitchen to hear anything that sounded like tears. I blew my nose, even though I was usually a person who didn't blow his nose.

Later, after I checked for red eyes in the mirror, I walked out to see her. She sat at the table, more absorbed in a newspaper than in the sounds of footsteps walking toward her. She didn't lift her face, not right away.

"Thank you." I held out my arms awkwardly, as if they weren't already attached to my shoulders, a Frankenstein boy. I wanted her to see that the sleeves were long enough. They went past my wrists, a first, onto the edges of my hands. I'd been growing so fast.

"You're welcome."

"I had no idea you even liked her or cared."

Which was true. Every time I put on Laura Nyro, my mother would remark on the wailing as if I'd chosen to fill up the bedroom wing with a fire siren instead of the sound of a human voice. *Christmas and the Beads of Sweat? New York Tendaberry?* Again?" No music was good enough unless it was classical; evoked discipline, control; conjured up a bygone era. I'd assumed that Joni and Laura had lived under the same roof for her. And she was the one who sat on the top.

She pushed at her teeth with the back of her tongue. "There's a lot about me you don't know."

She looked at the shirt on me, the placket, the collar, her eyes reconceiving me as a mannequin for a second. She mentioned that the shirt might look nice with my dungarees, and I pretended to agree. What I couldn't say was that I already knew that I'd never wear the shirt, at least not outside the house. I didn't want to be Joni—that idea came a while back, like a message without words. I wanted something more difficult. And it wasn't what you'd think. It had little to do with gender or how I dealt with being a boy. To follow Joni's lead was to find out what was inside me, which was a lot harder to find than I had the ability to see. On many days it felt like there was nothing there. I'd grab around to see if I could catch something, and I didn't know what to do with that. Who had taken me away from myself? What had I given up?

But I couldn't tell my mother any of that now—that would have been mean. If she'd been a different kind of mother, I would have hugged her, but you don't touch hurt people—she'd signaled that to me a long way back when I had tried to put my arms around her. She'd lost her twin brother, Paul, tragically and had never quite recovered. Think of giving a stray animal love, its heart growing so big after deprivation that the ache of touch could break open its ribs, killing it.

Instead, we sat together at the table. I didn't look at her face but down at her fingers, rougher than they had been when I was younger, a pinpoint-sized scab beside a fingernail. I pictured her pulling the fabric through the stabbing needle, hooded lamp on, hot. Her eyes.

SWEET BIRD

~~~~~

IF MUSIC WAS THE CLOSEST THING TO HOLINESS THAT I KNEW, then it couldn't stay inside an album cover for long. It couldn't be an artifact inside a sleeve. The bird inside had to be released. It had to fly around the room, go out the window, and come back in. It had to fill up time and space with its voice. To leave a mark, a stain of sound on the ceiling, sofa cushions, walls, floor.

In other words, if I loved a piece of music, I couldn't keep it to myself. If a friend of mine came over, they listened—they were *forced* to listen. Otherwise, it was like holding on to a secret, and I never did so well with secrets. To be alone with a secret turned me into a little bit of a monster, the music itself a monster. It was one thing to be in a one-to-one relationship with *The Hissing of Summer Lawns*, another thing entirely to open it up. And maybe that drive wasn't just about drawing nearer to my friend, though that was a part of it. I wanted to relearn the music all over again through my friend. Not just from listening to him catalogue his favorite moves, but from watching him interpret them in real time, seeing what they did to his face, hands, and arms. Did he look up at that crack in the ceiling when Joni hit that low note? Could he feel that key change in his solar plexus? Did he rearrange himself in the chair, cross one leg over the other, forehead rugged in thought? Would it make him shake his foot, even irregularly?

Listening together was a way to touch someone without ever having to extend a finger.

~~~~~

My bedroom looked more like the bedroom of a child now that the two of us were eighteen and looked more like men. It was 1978. The twin beds, the oak dresser, and the chest of drawers— they were bought during an era in which the world described itself more simply. They meant *boy* at a time when *pink baby blanket* meant *girl*. A narrative of a life was already implied by this furniture, even though I'd grown up in a house in which behaving like a boy hadn't come with the typical gender expectations. There were no chairs, so the two of us were seated together, side by side on the bed I slept on. I felt exceedingly conscious of every small move I made. Stomach noises, deep. Little groans. Whose were they?

With the door closed, the room felt tight, stuffy, the ceiling a little too low. But I couldn't keep it open with my mother, who couldn't stop herself from listening, in the house. She didn't want to miss out, and maybe she knew too well what could happen and didn't know how she would stop it, as she liked Albert. She'd always made him feel welcome in the house because he was kind to her and smart. He'd been at the top of our high school class and was off to a fancy private university in Connecticut this fall. Full scholarship.

I shook the album out from the sleeve and lifted it onto the spindle. There was a sound of planes taking off, the musical equivalent in horns. Then a sheen—polished, lacquered, expensive. It tricked you into thinking everything from here on out was going to be slick, but there was too much life underneath that surface, too many fissures, caves, and canyons. It wasn't operating from any script, which meant you had to do some work if you were going to be its listener.

I felt Albert looking at me even though he was staring straight ahead. He seemed to sense what his listening meant, as if by sitting there, he'd be hearing not who I was now but what I could be if I went on the long climb of finding it.

There was obedience in his face, his posture, his slouching shoulders, which looked like an old man's shoulders, endearing in someone who was only eighteen. He felt like a tourist to childhood, a visitor. That and his nubby gold cardigan, his leanness, his balding head and beard, thick dark hair sprouting from the collar of his Oxford shirt, the ends of sleeves, and all the places I couldn't see but wanted to.

Albert looked down at the lyrics.

"'Guesses based on what each set of time and change is touching,'" he said without context, both interested and neutral. He didn't lift his head but kept it down, as if studying for an exam.

He said it once more, testing out the sound in his mouth. No other offering. I couldn't tell whether he was in awe or found it pretentious. Maybe a little bit of both, and he couldn't hold on to two options at once. Or maybe he wasn't listening to the music at all but thinking about what would happen if he gave into his greatest reservation, which was to let down his guard, giving me the signal that he was ready for something back from me. Testing the queasy, electrified fence between friend and boyfriend, which I was scared of too, but it appeared to be a bigger deal for him. If he let go of all the rules that held him—and us—together, what would the next step be? Would he stop talking to me if I said the wrong thing or reached out to hold on to his leg?

It didn't occur to me that I held a lot of the power in the room. It was easier to think of myself as the one who was scrambling for it. But I was the one with feeling, which I experienced as vulnerability, though it wasn't. I was the one with the song in the largest sense. I knew what it was to be alive, which he would have killed for. If I were a cowbell, he could have shaken me out on the back step, and the clapper would have rung and rung and rung.

By this time I was writing music, liturgical music, publishing it in a monthly magazine with bright yellow-and-orange graphics that reflected some aspect of a sexy post-hippie sun in the style of Sister Corita Kent. Most of the songs in the issue didn't look like they'd been toiled over for years. They were likely written by someone who had picked up music within the last month, learned the configurations for five guitar chords (three major and two minor), and, in a burst of enthusiasm, used the text of a psalm as a starting-off point. They sounded like they were made to be strummed, not picked. Every element was rushed about such music, as if the songs were written out of the belief that the church would ban them for sedition at any minute and consign them to oblivion. Who had time for craftsmanship when people were trying to end racism, hunger, poverty, war—all things that these songs secretly wanted to impart to their audience? It was 1978, though most of the writers lived as if it were still the 1960s, not the era of Donna Summer and the Sex Pistols. The assembly's part was short, designed to be memorized after one rehearsal, without a song sheet. Sometimes too many syllables crammed into a verse as a way to retain some pattern on the verge of disintegration. Amateurism, approachability, drew me to these songs. They were short enough for a child's mind, even though I usually put away childish things.

One was laid out on the dresser, and as soon as Albert saw it, I was possessed of a desire to tear it out of his hands, but it was already too late. He studied its melody and chords for a while as if he were trying to translate the notes and words into music. It wasn't a very good song. Perhaps its one strength was that it did what some of Joni's songs did, in that it didn't begin on the dominant chord but the tonic. It lifted and defied your expectations at its threshold. But the chords had none of her spikes and textures. They were too smooth, resolved. They were easy to play, too easy. That was why it had ended up in this magazine for church musicians, who needed simple, elemental music so they could teach the congregation to sing robustly in one or two quick tries. It was a song that no one could love, a song that no one could hate either. Middle place. Muddy.

Albert closed the magazine and called me a genius. He said it with a kind of sadness that sounded like it was less about himself than it was about me, his concern for me. My gut-level response?

No. *No.* Don't say that to me. Let me earn it first. The song in front of him did not deserve that word, wasn't ready for someone as smart as he was to give it a grade. Yet I had conspired to put it out into the world. Why? To throw my name as far from myself as I could? To imply I existed, at the risk of my name coming back home to scoff at my laziness? I hadn't sat with it long enough, hadn't twisted it inside out to check every corner for a possible fix. I didn't want to live in a world that could give out that word so easily, even though he meant well, meant love to me. I could do so much better.

Meanwhile, people in pews were practicing that song in Northern California, in Chicagoland, in Florida, in Nova Scotia. Most were probably just fine with it in that it sounded like so many other songs. The world's engine is predictability. It keeps us from getting too hungry, and no one should be diminished or derided for eating its food. Undoubtedly, most were not looking at my name or caring that the words and music came from the hands of a single person. Perhaps those people felt and saw things in the song that I didn't see, and this was the thing I had to contend with. The director, the singers, the people in the congregation—they were looking at the black marks on the page and turning visual marks into sound, filling the room with spirit and breath, giving life to the air. They were trying their best to be in sync, and it's very hard to stay in sync. Multiple people aren't wired to match their voices to one melody—harmony camouflages that. They were trying to get the words down. They were trying to pull so many tasks together in real time, as the clock ticked. It was an act of alignment in motion, and the trick was to make sure it didn't sound like the labor of a construction team but a simultaneous action. As if it had arrived from outside of their exertions.

The point was, the song was no longer mine when it ended up in others' mouths, when it was powder on the tips of their fingers. The people in these churches also had their minds on sweeter things than the work of singing, such as what kinds of pastries were laid out on the table in the vestibule and whether they'd get to slip out after communion, in time for a cinnamon doughnut.

~~~~~

And one day the guitar, which had for so long been my secondary instrument, edged out piano. It didn't take long for it to change me down to the cellular level, to turn me into a creature that was much more social than I'd been, whether I'd wanted to be or not.

A piano provided a safe hiding place for the human body, but a guitar? When you stood in front of a group, a guitar made you vulnerable. Anyone could watch your legs, feet, torso, and arms. On top of that, its shape felt human. Its curves felt female or maybe the kind of guy with a big butt. Strummed and played at waist level, it announced itself as a phallus—and big. Didn't the guitar make everyone cooler, sexier, regardless of gender? Not just when your fingers were moving across the strings or twisting the pegs but when the guitar was carried in a case, slung over your back. The keyboard dominated the person who played it with its sheer size and weight, while the guitar was light—it had that *hole*. It was always telling you it wanted to be filled. It was waiting for you, for your fingers. It never let you forget that you had a waist. It rubbed against your belt buckle and zipper, letting you know that as soon as you lifted it over your head, it was hungry, ready to be touched again.

It was one of the most potentially embarrassing instruments, but what isn't embarrassing when you're a late teenager? Pulling down the shade is embarrassing. Going out to the kitchen to eat some cheese and crackers is embarrassing. Yawning is embarrassing. Peeing. Sitting down to pee. Everything was so fraught with embarrassment, it was no wonder I was determined to be proficient at the guitar, even though my index finger didn't have the strength for bar chords, unlike Joni, who must have had incredible flexibility in her knuckles and wrist despite polio. I couldn't get the buzz out of F-sharp minor chords, and the tips of my fingers were hot and sore from the heavy-gauge strings I used. It hadn't occurred to me I could switch to light, extra-light, as if such a move were cheating. I knew for sure I'd always be a keyboard player first, but I wouldn't be walking alongside my Joni if I didn't try to take a look around.

~~~~~

As I was learning the songs from *The Hissing of Summer Lawns* by heart, Bob Dylan and Sam Shepard put out *Renaldo and Clara*, their four-hour film, which never made it to the General Cinema Corporation's multiplex in the Cherry Hill Mall. Its main project was to record the Rolling Thunder Revue, two concert tours spotlighting not just Dylan but other performers in his orbit: Joan Baez, David Blue, Allen Ginsberg, Ronee Blakley, Harry Dean Stanton, and, of course, Joni. It bombed with both audiences and critics, who took a special pleasure in skewering its inconsistency, its "conflicting impulses to repress and reveal," as the *New York Times* put it. Only the most messianic Dylan fan might be drawn to it, its loose, inscrutable structure interspersed with improvised sketches suggested by Dylan's life and songs (who in the film *wasn't* some version of his wife, Sara?), but there are outtakes that shine, one moment in particular that captured Joni ablaze.

In that moment, Joni sits by Dylan's side, the two of them wielding their guitars, strumming with urgency. Roger McGuinn, once of The Byrds, is between them, a few feet in the background, in Gordon Lightfoot's living room. The wallpaper surrounding them crowded with flowers, magnified to psychedelic proportions. The animating face is McGuinn's. He is unwittingly playing the part of the professor, the rock and roll ambassador, translator of Joni's worth to the viewer. Maybe he is translating it for Dylan too, who, beneath his fur hat, refuses to be too impressed. He keeps his eyes down, appearing to be involved in "Coyote," Joni's newest song, but doesn't give us any sense that he approves of it, or finds it exceptional or anything palpably different from what Joni's done before, notably *Court and Spark*, which reportedly caused him to feign sleep when she played the finished version for him along with a group of others at David Geffen's house. Dylan long ago shut the lights off on any signs of openness and legibility, maybe figuring out that mystery was central to his appeal. Who would Bob Dylan be without mystery? "Mr. Mystery," Joni addressed him in a song written during this time. In this way, he might have been like the withholding father born of the traits of patriarchy, even though his work wanted to skewer that figure again and again. What would his work be without this skewering? By writing and playing, was he trying to hate it out of himself?

None of this withholding stops Joni—her voice and playing only get harder, more urgent. The director's camera comes in closer to capture every nuance, every flicker-signal of simultaneous, contradictory emotion. Her face is vigilant. She seems to know that Dylan isn't going to give her what she wants and needs—that is an old story between them—but that doesn't stop her from pushing. Maybe the meticulousness of her work is a big fuck-you to anyone who would put her in second place. Though she admits to being influenced by him, she is no longer singing for him but for music, which is a tougher but more appreciative god. And maybe she's trying to tell him that he's lazy, complacent, too easy on himself. His love for spontaneity is just an excuse for being settled. Would he even know how to play a chord with a note outside the triad? Or anything out of his four-chord limit? Would he care?

Joni might not be seeing that the search for excellence can turn on itself. It can be a little too certain of its ideology. It can be a little too judgmental of the chaos and mess of life, and maybe some would see that impulse translated into her outfit, her bracelets and beret. She'd already taken flak for wearing Yves Saint Laurent pants, a quilted Chanel bag over her shoulder, dressing like a "Beverly Hills housewife," as she'd recall to Cameron Crowe in *Rolling Stone*. Her response? She'd spoof her critics by writing a song or two giving life to versions of this character. There's nothing about this performance that's less than an event, and maybe it concentrates on what it was like to be a woman in music in 1976, when every force around you wanted to diminish and fuck you. For all of his good intentions, Roger McGuinn plays the part of the wolf. He looks like he's simultaneously in love with the queen and wants to eat every part of her served up on fine china. Not just physically but her soul, which isn't the same thing as wanting to destroy her. Does he want to feed off her life force? The more you look at the video, the more menacing it seems beneath its exuberance, and that might be one way to describe the experience of Joni's song. Riptides hiding in calm waters.

⌁

In my bed one night, I imagined a parasail. The wing dragging me through the cold current of early summer, pulling the seat at high speed toward the drawbridge pylon, salty and corroded with protruding iron rods, orange with rust. Would it lift? I tensed my arms and legs for the crash. Genius? *Not so fast.* I went through the song he looked through, pored over the others I'd written and published. Their melodies were blocky. They weren't in sync with the rhythms of my speaking patterns, not only in terms of the dispersal but the reach of its melody. It didn't believe that words were central. A song didn't have to do astounding things to be a good song. It didn't have to change keys or meter; it didn't need to pivot around an unorthodox chord. Great songs are written inside the constraint of four chords. Dylan songs, of course. Neil Young songs. Dolly Parton: "I Will Always Love You." I loved that song. Heard it for the first time in a Howard Johnson's motel in Port Allen, Louisiana, the night before our family dropped off my brother to start his freshman year at LSU. Were we abandoning him? Would we see him again? The question went both ways. The song was made of the simplest elements, but each note shimmered with an unexpected complexity. Each note mattered. I could almost forget that the singer was dumping the *you* of the song. Its tender declaration might have also been a way for the singer to appear selfless and exemplary not just to the *you* but to herself.

But I was putting songs out there that I didn't care enough about to have strong feelings for. If they'd been brutalized in a workshop for indulging in major 7th chords, the default signature of cocktail-lounge jazz, I wouldn't have flinched or cried. I would have written another one but better. I hadn't lived with any of them long enough to discover anything fresh inside their folds, something I hadn't known before. They hadn't taught me anything back. And this was genius? Maybe he was insulting me.

But Albert's voice was too tender to be an insult. And he had no reason to hurt me other than to push me away, and when it came time to push me away, he found other ways to do it. Later he told our mutual friend Holly that I was immature, and Holly of course would report that back to me, not with any frame or context but because she thought it was her duty to protect me by telling me what he was hiding from me. She thought that this information would show me how much stronger emotionally I was than Albert. And maybe she hadn't foreseen how much this would hurt me, not so much that he'd say such a thing but that he'd feel it strongly enough to report it to her in the first place. *Immature*: synonym for *weakness*. *Immature*: *childish, babyish, soft, crude, green, puerile, wet behind the ears*. I made lists of all the things I thought of as immature. *Unsexy*? *Unsexy*. That's where it hit me; that's where I felt it, between my legs. Not as a moral failing, but I felt that too. An immature person didn't know how to look beyond the limits of self, ego, his needs. Was that how he saw me? Did Holly think that too?

I threw off the covers on my bed. The moon came in through

the window, the moon I called Melissa because it terrified me when I was young, and what better to do with something that scares you than give it a name of your choosing, a name that's friendly, even a little commonplace, nerdy. How did *immature* square with *genius*? They sounded like two animals scrabbling around in a cage, one running around in circles, the other hunkering in a lump, eyes shut, waiting for the day it would be let out the door. The genius couldn't stand the look of the immature and thus banged on the bars. Did one win over the other? Did one take a bite out of the other? Or did they consign themselves to living side by side, putting up with each other's habits, matters of eating and grooming techniques, coming into a pact that they'd take the best from each other?

At least the immature animal still believed in light, change. In the possibility of the moon spreading light over his forehead while he slept.

In the morning, I was about to get out of bed when a song sparrow sang from outside, just a few feet away from my head on the pillow. It sounded like no other song sparrow I'd ever heard, and my gut feeling was to freeze, to keep it from flying off the rose trellis. Certainly it could hear my every movement, my feet on the sheets, the back of my scalp on the pillow. It sung its three-note pattern, trilled—then went silent. Three-note pattern, trill, silence. The wind through the window smelled of marsh, its eggy, sulfurous tang half-life, half-death. The longer I listened to the sparrow, the more I sensed it wanted another bird, someone similar, to acknowledge him. And not just for company but to sing the same song back. But the sparrow only heard blowing branches and the distant whir of the causeway. A car went by, and then another. A fire siren went off in the distance, in another town. Linwood? The answer wasn't coming to him any time soon. But that didn't mean he stopped singing.

~~~~~

When I asked my mother if I could help out with dinner or laundry, she shook her head. She didn't let us forget that she felt bored and burdened by those tasks, but they were hers, they were her arena of care, and none of us knew what our house would be if we started rearranging the words we used to categorize ourselves—*mother*, *father*, *child*, *brother*. Her pupils contracted; the amber flecks in her iris floated in watery green. We were all in a box not of our making. We were all lifting our utensils to our mouths and drinking sweetened iced tea at the kitchen table. What if a box could be a chord, and we allowed a dissonant note to make us put our forks down and dream? What if we put an F in the root when the chord above it was C major 7? Would it change us? Would we still know how to stand up, take care of ourselves, when it was time we moved on from one another?

~~~~~

Months later two objects sat side by side atop my bedroom dresser: the cover of *The Hissing of Summer Lawns* and a magazine in which my song appeared.

Inside the album, Joni floated on her back in the pool behind her Bel-Air house. She wasn't naked as she was in the *For the Roses* shot but in a gray bikini this time, eyes closed but not squeezed shut. She wasn't pulling herself through the water. She didn't appear to be pushing, thinking, looking outward. It would be a mistake to think she was looking for anything, and even if she was, the expression on her face didn't suggest she thought it was above or below her. It was the face of peace, which might come from the other side of experience, perspective, meditation. Or was this what a teacher of mine referred to as a Valium haze? Initially I felt panic because the image was pretending that that panic didn't exist. It wasn't calming either, and you'd only think it was calming if you were a person who didn't want to think.

Whereas *For the Roses* felt personal, *Hissing* felt cinematic, or rather like a series of short movies in which Joni played the various roles that made this image possible, which was why it didn't feel narcissistic. There was something here about wealth. Something about ennui, emptiness, surfaces, traps, lies, secrets, violence, oppression, willed forgetfulness, racism, the brutality and arbitrariness of America. It looked expensive, but it believed that that expensiveness was a false god.

These weren't the kind of songs that made you say, *I love this song.* There was a tension between the polished surface and the rawness of the lyrics, as well as with the restrained chaos in them. The women protagonists were all in trouble—sometimes they knew that; more often they didn't. There wasn't a boring note on the album. There were more instruments than ever, a slicker production than her earliest albums but still raw underneath, like fish that had been seared. The same weird bones, the open chords, the unexpected harmonic movements—were the songs even rooted in a key? They didn't even seem to be interested in keys. They began in one place and ended somewhere else, with no compulsion to return to the beginning. And if they did return to the beginning, they were made richer by that move. They wanted to astonish you, but you had to give them your full attention—you had to move along with the song to be humbled, astonished. Words were at the center of this experience, which is why they weren't heightened with broad melodic leaps. And when you searched for and found Easter eggs, you felt chosen, a little special for having put in the time. You knew most of it would go over other people's heads. It was the song that many would skip while playing the record.

Again and again I thought, *This is a person who makes up her own rules, then follows them, and when they stop serving the music, she breaks them down and makes better rules.* If there were a god of this music, it was the god of meticulousness, specificity, details, brushstrokes. And it never felt like she was competing with other music. If she was competing, it was with her own high standards. I wrote something down that Jung said: "No other way is like yours. All other ways deceive and tempt you. You must fulfill the way that is in you."

~~~~~

As for my song in the magazine? It was much more involved than anything I'd written before. I'd been patient against at least five tries when I believed it was dead, but just when I was about to give up, it had become another creature. All it took was the movement of a sixth in the refrain, just where the key changed before it slipped back into its original pattern.

I could have laughed at the clarity of the choices in front of me, one route or the other. I hadn't set it up to behave like that, but it was all there, as if the binary had taken on a life of its own. Straight versus gay, woman versus man, country versus city, water versus rock, raw versus cooked, god versus devil.

God of cruelty. God of delight.

The world had fallen in love with its pain way back—that was plain enough. It cultivated that in its language and laws and wars and sent it out through people, who lived and died with its consequences until they decided they'd had enough and stood up.

I cleared the top of the dresser, put the magazine and album away. The real truth was that I was ashamed of God, embarrassed about being associated with anything having to do with God. God did too much harm in the world, I knew that. Too often humans used that name to justify domination, genocide, racism, cruelty, piracy, and theft, and to look good while they were doing it. Did Joni have a god? She took pains to balk at the name of God in her songs, but God was always on her mind. God leaked into the lyrics, as if through the finest cracks in the porcelain. "You need to believe in something. . . ." Once God was love for her, and then that transferred to art. All of her songs said art mattered, which made sense when the body of romance and sex let you know at every turn that it had limits. It aged, it got tired, and it couldn't be relied upon to draw others to you.

Maybe I knew that the word had different associations for me than it did for others, especially those who used God as a weapon against anyone who didn't look or sound like them. For me? God wasn't hardness. God didn't have a human form. God was too large to be confined by a book that attempted to describe God;

God was too fluid and tricky to be chained to a name, to genders, to a body. God, in purest form, was music. Love, sex, ocean, animals, trees. God was kindness, plus every benevolent force that deserved to live beyond confinement. That was it: sweet bird. *The sky.* Because at every turn, confinement was lurking, even when you thought you'd busted through its bars.

AMELIA

~~~~

THE CARS OUTSIDE THE MANN MUSIC CENTER WERE PACKED SO
tight, I couldn't open the passenger door. I looked over the hood
at the car parked ahead of us—so many sedans, station wagons,
vans. For weeks I thought I'd imagined the concert so intricately
that I could have already seen and heard it—the setlist, her outfit, the postures of the band members, how they hunched into
their instruments while picking or threw their heads back or
made those hotdogging expressions that verged on embarrassing
if they weren't already fully there. I saw how she leaned over
the edge of the stage to the girl lifting the cone of red roses. It
hadn't occurred to me that there would be people, so many people, between our seats and the stage. This was a crowd, hepped
up, with personalities that had wants and concerns that were
different from my own.

"Boxed in," I said.

"You don't approve of my parking?" Holly said, genuinely
offended.

I jerked up on the handle. There was all of six inches between the passenger door and the car next to me.

"Car's too close," I said. "I think you need to back out and pull in all over again."

Only a half hour ago, I'd leapt across the front lawn with such finesse, I might have been a flying pony on amphetamines. I'd let loose such a ridiculous animal sound that the kid across the street, who had been hosing down his black TransAm, scowled his derision. Now I didn't want to move.

"Climb over. Come on," she said, pointing to the stick shift knob. "You can do it."

And so I did: an approximation of a yoga plank pose just so I wouldn't injure private parts.

We walked forward. Around us people were straggling, lighting up the bowls of their pipes, skunking up the air with weed—others couldn't wait to get to their seats. Someone lugged a cardboard cutout of a yellow taxi that was so sloppy and childish in its conception, I winced and looked away.

I was sure my life was about to change. In so many ways, Joni had been more dream to me than actual person, a facet of my interiority. I couldn't tell the two of us apart any more than I could distinguish the vision in my left eye from my right. I'd harvested the best parts of her mind. Only the broadest markers suggested we were different: she oriented herself to the Pacific, I the Atlantic. She called herself a flatlander while I was a creature of the marsh. She probably had a lot of sex; I *thought* all the time about a life in which I had a lot of sex. The idea of her having moving hands, arms, and a face slowed down my walk, as if I'd aged forty years in twenty feet. For so long she was the only sound in my ears.

She wasn't very visible in 1979, five years after *Court and Spark*'s Top 10 success. It didn't take much to be past peak as a pop musician, as if long careers were sugar maples in Vermont past the third week of September. Some mixed reviews, others crushing; dwindling record sales; little to no airplay. It was just a part of the mulching of the business, the next tree growing out of the rotten bark of the past. Once she was on the cover of *TIME* magazine, and now I never came across any articles or interviews about her in the papers. The lone exception was Cameron Crowe's cover profile in *Rolling Stone*, which I always kept in a visible place in my bedroom, rotating its position every few weeks. I read it so many times that I likely could be quizzed upon it and win a special prize. The comment about her parents as "old-fashioned and moral people." Her interest in clothes: walking around Saskatoon in a hat and gloves. The thought that she'd have gone into women's wear if the music thing hadn't panned out. Her mother telling a neighbor that Joan had left for New York City to become a musician, and the neighbor telling her, "Oh, you poor woman."

In truth, I also wanted to know who Joni was outside the frame of the songs. Who was this person so gifted and evolved that she could make "Winn-Dixie cold cuts" sound like exquisite things, jewels in a painting? Every description came with a frame around it, and the frames never overcrowded the wall like some antique store in which no one had bought anything in a dozen years. I could see and remember each image after I heard it—each one mattered but not too much. And somehow she made these songs while living some approximation of an everyday life with a housekeeper named Dora; personal assistants; Elliot Roberts, her manager; Henry Lewy, her trusty engineer—okay. But what did she eat for breakfast and for snacks? Peanut butter crackers or cream cheese and olives? Was she the kind of person who chatted up the cashier in the checkout line? Did she send Christmas cards to her dentist and doctor? Was she a lousy driver? And did she pick up after herself or leave all those dirty dishes to the beleaguered Dora? Dora, who told her to "have children," as she said in "Song for Sharon," as if such a thing would make a grown-up woman of her.

Maybe not a single thing about her lined up. Something about that made my face a little hot but excited me too.

I thought I bought tickets close enough to the stage, but here we were, so high, so far back, it was practically the rafters. I looked down over the tiers of seats, the semicircle they made, the hot blue-and-red lights of the stage. At least there was a roof over our heads. Better that than to sit behind others on the lawn, what was tactfully called general admission, but was closer to half-assed chaos. From here the roadies on the stage had no features. My contact lens prescription wasn't strong enough; it wasn't correcting anything beyond five rows. No hard lines. Once Joni was out there with her band, I wouldn't even be able to tell how tall she was. I *thought* she was tall, but I read somewhere that she was five foot six, and that had to be an error. I'd tower over her by, what—eight inches? If that was true, I'd have to sit down, stay down.

As for the other concertgoers, they were older than we were, years into their adult lives, with careers, maybe kids. They probably had lots of sex if they weren't bored of each other yet. There was good cheer about them, as if seeing Joni would be a fun thing to do together on a Friday night, a memory they'd talk about in the future to their friends, kids, and grandkids. Among these people there had to be someone who was as dedicated to Joni as much as

I was. They knew by heart the lyrics to "Dreamland," "Blonde in the Bleachers," and "The Priest," but if they didn't, they kept themselves disguised under Foster Grants, the sunglasses of the day. I saw no fretful faces, no moistened lips. No one in a state like I was in, pinning my arms to my sides so no one could see the sweat rings.

Certainly Holly and I must have talked; we must have speculated as to what songs she'd sing, what we wanted to hear, how big the band would be, who was playing—all of that. But I must not have been altogether present. I had all the absorbent properties of a high-end paper towel, which is not the same thing as being an interpreter. I felt a little sick. I thought I might have thrown up if I'd had the strength to suffer the shame. Instead, I sat in my seat, hands underneath my thighs, waiting for something wet to fall down on me from above.

~~~~

My brother and I sat in the sunroom, beneath the hole in the ceiling, the hole our father had pulled open years ago after the tiles had started to drip during storms. A ring of overlapping stains hadn't been enough for him. He had to get to the source, and in doing so, he exposed the guts of the house, tufts of insulation as pink as cotton candy on a paper cone, sweet enough to eat, if not for the filaments finer than broken glass. The day on which he'd get around to fixing it was long ago in the past. Our family no longer had the ability to see it unless we had a visitor, whose eyes went right to that spot. Then at last we felt like the secrets we'd been trying to hide were all out there, all there for them to see.

The morning after the concert, Bobby had his mind on going

back to LSU, and I must have felt I had a duty to cheer him up—or at least distract him. I can't imagine he was asking me about the concert, but occasionally he let on that he'd been listening to Joni's songs from his bedroom down the hall with more attention than I had given him credit for, quoting a description from "Refuge of the Roads." I told him there wasn't a note that wasn't impeccable, no missed words, no intonation problems in the upper register. There wasn't any gap between what I expected and how she performed, and at the same time, she never phoned it in. She wasn't singing the same phrases she sang at Merriweather Post or Forest Hills, the other stops on the tour—I could tell. With each phrase, I felt her pushing herself toward a threshold.

And—oh—the piano cadenza in "The Last Time I Saw Richard," which made it sound like she'd tumbled it through the long solo from the middle of "Paprika Plains"—a recent era. Such wide-open chords, as if she'd closed her eyes, let go, and become Debussy.

I suppose I was using Bobby to make the memory last, to tattoo it not just onto the underside of my brain but onto his as well. And I described the setlist, songs he might have known or not. "In France They Kiss on Main Street," "Edith and the Kingpin," "Coyote." I was intricately describing how she performed each song, how they differed in subtle ways from the recorded version, a horn on this one, an inverted chord on that one, one measure shifting into a disco beat and back to its original 4/4 rhythm. And by the time I got to "Goodbye Pork Pie Hat"—well, I didn't sing it for my brother. Singing would have been an act of intimacy. Singing would only have come from feeling safe with and trusting each other, but I must have spoken the last line and used my hands the way Joni used her hands: to emphasize the flashing of a neon sign. Hand gestures that looked like I had glitter hidden in my palms, which I threw back toward his face. It was one of the few songs she sang back then without holding her guitar, and if you've built a career out of singing and playing an instrument, you don't have to think about your hands; your hands are always moving, occupied, foundational. Without that prop, you were on your own. I wasn't sure whether Joni was comfortable with making a language of her hands, but she was making every effort to look like she was, as if she'd spent years studying Sarah Vaughan's phrasing in the little jazz clubs of the Upper West Side.

And that did it. Bobby stomped out of the room. Whatever he said was lost in the stomping, but his actions said, *You look like an idiot.*

Or worse: *Love turned you into a stupid idiot.*

If I was going to tattoo him, he was going to do it back, but this time get underneath a larger bank of skin in a color and place I didn't want. It rushed underneath the surface like blood, so hot that it needed ice cubes, a cooling washcloth. It was breathtaking to be taken down like that, stunning when I wasn't girded for it. What did I do that set him off like that? That I wasn't reading the room, the marks of ambivalence on his face? That I wasn't thinking about him heading back to Baton Rouge, where he'd live on the high floor of a dorm with windows that didn't open? That I could love something so much, I didn't care if I was making a fool of myself? We were a family that loved things—some would say too much. Especially my siblings. Against our parents' chaos and need for control—hobbies? No, love was the only word. Our love gave us perspective. Love told us there was more to life than our sad, constricted house. Love was a way out: a world out there. Bobby and his pieces of mid-century furniture, Michael and his photographic knowledge of lost department stores. Maybe this kind of love needed to be held close to oneself. Privacy was central to that love, and I'd gone and violated some pact meant to be protected, unspoken. I had the audacity to suggest that we could be different. We could be more honest and less afraid of each other.

I didn't go looking for him in his bedroom afterward. Likely he was as embarrassed as I was now and didn't understand why he'd exploded either. I could have said, *Hey, why did you walk away from me like that? Don't worry, I'm not mad at you.* But sense could not be found in our disruption. We weren't a family in which conversations like that could take place, could grapple toward some resolution. There was a box that held us in place even though we couldn't see the box.

My cousin Andy looked out at us from behind the lectern. His hands, big, with a Band-Aid on one knuckle, grabbed on to the sides of it. We were all at the church to celebrate the life of his mother, my aunt Anna, who had died within the last few weeks, but he was talking as much about himself as if it were impossible not to do that when he had been snuffed out for so long. He'd walked to the altar at a point so late in the funeral mass that nobody, much less the priest, thought to grab his arm and say, *Hey, be still.* Grief had made a monster of him. It torqued occasional words to indecipherable pronunciations. It caused him to put on a suit that was a size or two too big for him. He was already a blocky man, the gap between his shirt and the collar and the length of his sleeves only made him look blockier, like the Frankenstein monster I'd been afraid of as a kid, with my fear that he was looking into the bedroom window late at night. When I looked at Andy's face—aviator glasses, thin lips, dark hair parted and combed to the side—I imagined him as the guy whom people forgot to see when he walked into a room before apologizing. He was the guy whom people called Alfred, Jose, Herb, Stewart, Clark—any name but his own name, and after a while, he stopped correcting them. What was the point when people didn't like you to push too hard? It was easier to go undetected sometimes. Part of it was his low, inward-turning light, which he might have cultivated over time out of a need to protect himself.

But nothing was as unsettling as the way he looked at us, not as a whole group but as individuals. I felt my aunts and cousins looking away or down when his eyes fell to them. He seemed to capture everyone in the room, not just once or twice but several times. That act was as important as the words that came out of his mouth. It was his method: dividing and conquering. When he looked at me, I was already in practice—I wasn't going to look away. This didn't mean he didn't embarrass me or that I felt a duty to support him. It was just that I wasn't going to give him what he wanted, and maybe I wasn't very much in favor of the idea of him using *his* grief to take center stage. His siblings were in the front row. His aunts and uncles behind them. The story of Aunt Anna was complicated. My relatives spoke about her as if she'd been dying for decades, someone who'd gotten so big with sadness that the sadness had trapped her in her five-room house, and this gathering had been a forgone conclusion, imagined by them for years. But that didn't mean that there wasn't genuine pain in the room. People were missing her, as well as all the others in their lives who had died, which is the way of all funerals. And all the deaths to come, not to mention their own.

It was the first time I'd ever seen him, but then again I barely saw any of his siblings, all of whom were from a different generation. He was old enough to be my father but younger than my own. The word was that he'd worked at Macy's, lived in New York City, which was a synonym for a wasted, shitty life—he could have been something. He could have married, fathered children instead of spending all of his money on rent. He never came back home for holidays or family celebrations, and the blame seemed to fall on him, even though he was probably never invited. Mostly no one had talked about him. It was too shameful to talk of his disappointment, the tacit assumptions of depravity—the oldest of his siblings, someone who had forsaken the duty to set an example, and rather than help care for his ailing mother, he'd run away. The ninety miles to Manhattan might have been nine hundred, the length of a round-trip plane ticket in emotions.

He blundered and started again. He knew, without a doubt, that this was the great moment of his life, but he hadn't taken any notes, nor had he practiced before the mirror last night. He was all over the place. Strong emotions are of no help to us when it comes to telling a coherent story. They're at best sung, and maybe that was why every second sentence kept coming back to a phrase: *simple Slovak woman*. Simple Slovak woman. It had a musical quality, the repetition. There was a metronome inside it, and each utterance ended up standing in for ten minutes of talk.

He simply could have said it twenty-five times in a row, and it would have been his song. Beautiful.

He said the phrase with affection, but I knew his words were meant to hook into the skin. And he spoke it as much about all of us, whether we were Slovak or women or not. He was calling us out for something larger than himself, larger than the sanctuary, and I wanted to say, *Oh, no you don't. Not me. I am not one of these rigid people; I'm changing. I have so much sidesplitting joy ahead, you have no idea. I'm already well into the next life. And for another thing . . .*

I bit into my cheek lining and held on until I tasted blood.

The problem was that I couldn't feel any connection to him. Since all he expected of us was betrayal, I was only going to give him betrayal. He was calling the shots.

At the same time, I couldn't let go of the pain in his eyes, his voice, his hands, his trunk, his feet. It look me a while. Embarrassment so thick—mine? His? A snow cloud took over the room, obscuring the truth. I knew he'd been hurt and was living with this hurt every day and even this great moment of his life was not going to repair any of it, and he already knew it while he was up there. At least he'd tried.

After mass we gathered at my other aunt's house. At some point within the last year or two, I'd stopped looking forward to the family gatherings—I didn't know what that was about. Was it simply the word *girlfriend*? Asked once or twice in a seemingly benign spirit? Just once or twice—that was enough to lay on the pressure, make it feel like a threat. I took a seat outside, beneath the messy tree, pushing seed pods around with my buffed shoes. In no time at all, Andy walked toward me, looking at me as if he'd picked me out—my face warming up, oh no, no you're not, you're not sitting here—and as soon as I gave an inner voice to that, I knew it would happen. It had happened. "Hi," he said, with a nervous, shy laugh, eyes on the curtains on the window behind me. "Hi," I said, laughing too, but muffled. And just at that moment, my uncle Joe sat down across from us, sweating Bud can in hand, as if he had the skill set to sense the awkwardness about to take place, and he knew exactly how to defuse it.

And what was that question he asked? *How was my music going?*

I talked about the songs I'd been writing, how I was writing more songs on the guitar, how I'd begun to use open tunings, how I was learning to get used to them, light-gauge strings being less likely to break, especially in performance. I told him I wasn't writing liturgical songs so much anymore, but I was still publishing the ones I'd written—I'd had a big backlog. I told him I'd stopped writing things down as a way to keep the songs in the air, alive before setting their feet in wet concrete. I'd gotten a four-track tape recorder—my father had given it to me for my birthday—and I was using it as much as I could, but reel-to-reel tape was expensive, and more often than not, I was erasing my previous work, not knowing if I was erasing the best of me. It felt better to keep making new versions of myself, throwing the old me away, ruthless, indifferent, like little murders.

Then I was talking about Joni: if only I could get a BA in Joni Mitchell, which I believed was hilarious, though neither of them registered it—probably they didn't know her from Joan Baez. It had taken me this long to process the concert, and I was still learning from it; I would always be learning. I knew I was going on longer than I should have, but I was riding an electric current, and it was easier to go on than to carry on an actual conversation that would have intruded on the uncomfortable with the inevitable questions. The messy tree, a mimosa, shook itself—or the wind did. At a certain point, Uncle Joe's gaze retreated back into his head, though I felt his steadiness beneath his worried brows, his rheumy eyes pink in the corners—he was trying to be a gentleman. Likely he was thinking about how to get himself another beer without breaking the voltage of our exchange.

All the while Andy fixed on me as if he could see right through every thought I'd had about him, and he wasn't bothered; he didn't mind the arrogance of my interpretations of him, even though some of them might have been accurate. He'd been in my shoes too. All gay people had to be like this—hypervigilant, curious, judging—just to survive everyday group encounters, in which someone was ever on the ready to use your observations against you. Roll their eyes, disagree reflexively, or sometimes a whole lot worse. No wonder we couldn't let go enough to draw closer in our relationships.

Then his face looked concerned, not for himself exactly but for me. *You can go now*, said the look in his eyes, brighter now, more involving and resigned than they'd been up on the lectern. *It's all right*. Then he lingered for a bit, just so that thought would touch the back of my mind.

And that was the last time I saw him. Andy.

Bethlehem, Pennsylvania: August 1979.

~~~~~

A nearby college ran a coffeehouse with an open mic, and though I dreaded the idea of putting myself in that situation, I thought I should do it. I thought it would be the stepping stone to playing in clubs, getting a regular gig—something that a legitimate performer was expected to do, even if you primarily thought of yourself as a songwriter. All my performances thus far had been in churches, schools, concerts with my high school peers—venues where there were already customs of listening with respect, or at least pretending to do so. It would be a different matter to perform in a coffeehouse, where people talked and laughed, walked in and walked out, spilled things, felt no compulsion to extend any respect to you. In fact, maybe that was part of the pact. It was part of proving yourself. Could you capture that audience when you followed, say, a stand-up comedian whom they had practically booed off the stage?

Luckily, I didn't follow any stand-up comedian, and instead of talking and walking out, the people listened to me sing my three originals, accompanied by guitar. Which didn't make this night any easier, as I sensed there was someone on the other side of the spotlight, a guy with wire glasses, faded denim shirt, and dark brown beard who saw through my songs, every last note where I was hiding. He could see I was avoiding pronouns. He could see the hours of labor that went into that avoidance, all the twisting circuitry that ended up making the song less immediate, less intimate. He knew that one small hiding made for bigger hiding. It affected my phrasing. It shaped how I handled the end of the refrain, which snapped off too soon because it didn't want to say the wrong thing. He knew that I wanted to puddle into the song, transform into a three-dimensional staff with a time signature and quarter notes in place of this human body, a male body not that many years out of puberty. Instead, I stood out here, exposed for anybody canny enough to see it. I wanted to be raw nerves the way Joni was raw nerves on the title song of *Blue*. But that was a different kind of exposure. That was generous. She was including us in her heartbreak. I, on the other hand, was keeping people out when I wanted to throw my arms around them.

There was applause, strong. I smiled as best I could, with the left corner of my mouth. When I stepped forward into the dark, I looked over at his side of the room, but his seat was empty, which didn't mean I didn't feel his presence following me out the door, sitting beside me in the front seat of my parents' station wagon, walking with me to the back door of our house. He even crawled into bed with me but knew I was afraid to touch him, so he rolled away to one side of the mattress to let me know it was my loss.

~~~

When I first listened to the album *Hejira* a couple years before, I was confused by so much: its static melodies, the indifference to unexpected harmonic shifts. Joni's wide-open chords still held the songs together, as did her words—which seemed to take precedence over the music. But Joni wasn't making full use of the style she'd been developing over the years. There were none of the vivid colors of her two previous albums, none of the multitrack choral parts that always conjured up brain waves for me. She seemed to be rejecting the possibility of the wider audience she'd cultivated for her work. No Top 40 songs were going to come from this material, even if "Coyote" was released as the lead single. She was robbing herself of her strengths in order to concentrate on territory she hadn't explored before—in this case, a consistently lower vocal register. Cooler atmospheres. A black-and-white movie at a time when color was the default.

But the music wouldn't let me go. If I wasn't actively listening to it, I was singing the songs in my imagination, in the car, or lying awake in the middle of the night. I wanted to get to the other side of bewilderment, which I experienced as an impediment: otherworldly rubble in the center of the road. I didn't know that bewilderment was just what the work wanted of me, and one day the songs would open themselves to me like a person I'd misread, somebody I'd mistaken as shut down when there was so much life inside.

In my memory of the concert, Joni's hands moved as if they'd done all the thinking themselves on the fingerboard, over the soundhole. They slapped the strings where the neck met the body—a percussive *tick*. This was *Hejira*'s "Amelia," a song that contended with aloneness. Hadn't she always been alone? The other musicians in the band knew better than to share the stage with her for this one.

She could disguise her aloneness from the audience by surrounding herself with musicians, brilliant musicians: Jaco Pastorius, Don Alias, Pat Metheny, Michael Brecker, Lyle Mays. But the person who wrote the song was alone, looking out at the desert and up to the sky and those vapor trails, which first appear as a figure from the *I Ching*, and next at the six strings of her guitar. She was lifting off, flying now, with nothing beneath her to support her, no net or parachute. Solo. No company, no lover, no community or friends. Which was why there wasn't any bass player to bolt the song to the ground, both live and on the recording. All treble.

What other song felt so deeply emotional, in an extended way, without ever making me cry? Crying, I suppose, came about from disruption. A song or poem touched something you hadn't seen coming, and it set you off, it broke you in two. "Amelia," on the other hand, was consistently astral, even when it was back to Earth at the end, at the desert-bound Cactus Tree Motel. It was baked in an atmosphere that was sad, ineffably so, but the song was oddly hopeful too, though it didn't declare itself as such. The speaker had touched something dark, but she lived. She survived—*is* surviving, unlike Icarus, who plunges to his death in the song. She was probably going to touch something dark again. She went forward with that but wasn't demolished by that knowledge, unlike the reachers of Greek myth.

How did she make you feel it? Maybe it was the trick of orienting you in one key, F, and lifting you up into another, G. When I sat down to listen to the song fully, I took away three chords. I knew there were extra notes in those three chords, but they didn't sound like the chords in *Court and Spark* and *Hissing*. For all of its allusions to flight, the melody limited itself to a six-note range, which was startling given the sublime range of "Car on a Hill" just two and a half years before. But the song was wily and a little secretive about that strategy. Maybe because the song was less about Amelia Earhart, whose desire to be the first woman in solo flight disappeared her, than it was about Joni, who lives. At this point in time, she was more interested in thinking about all the ways we were alone, all the ways we traveled with and developed psychic resilience through our losses.

And there she was at nine, airlifted from North Battleford to the polio clinic in Saskatoon. Far from home and friends, from parents. One hundred thirty miles away. Would she live? She couldn't even move if she had the energy to. Not even allowed to look down at the farms that passed beneath her as the engine drowned out her voice.

But there was more. Maybe she was processing the tension between expectation and the inevitable outcome, which is another way to say that life makes a mess of our attempts to corral and shape it. Life chastens our reaching, whether it comes to love or the songs we write. Even when disaster has been averted, life is pressing its thumbs into the wet clay of our stories, reshaping the narratives we live by even when we don't consciously think of them as *narratives*. Sometimes life leaves them in pieces: "picture postcard charms." Individual moments in time, disconnected from one another, without emotional logic or causality. A pot dropped to the floor. Shatter.

Could I make meaning of any of that when it was all I could do to worry songs into being in the middle of the night? Whenever I tried to write like Joni, it sounded at best like an outtake. Descriptions and guitar chords untested by life experience. I knew the route before I set out to explore. Before I could lose—and fail at—something, I needed to do something first. I needed to love someone, needed to lose myself, and I was behind on that, way behind, while everyone else seemed to know that there wasn't very much time. They made choices even though they might have known that they were the wrong choices. What would my love be? A person? A place? My music? To listen to this song was to listen to the life ahead of me—my death too. To mourn everything first—lost relationships, lost parents, lost places—as a way to prepare for my arrival.

~~~~~~~~~~~~~~~~~~~~

B
E
C
O
M
I
N
G

~~~~~~~~~~~~~~~~~~~~

MOON AT THE WINDOW

MY FRIEND AND COLLEGE CLASSMATE DENISE TALKED ABOUT THE Iowa Writers' Workshop as if there were no question I already knew every last thing about it—didn't everyone? She didn't mention that it was the top writing school in the country or that it was one of the most selective graduate programs in any field. Or that it was the program where Flannery O'Connor, James Tate, Rita Dove, and Joy Williams had gone to school. She'd wanted to be a fiction student there so badly that she decided not to put her completed application in the mail. Why? "A rejection," she said, only half in jest, "would destroy me." For her it was healthier to remove the conditions for that no. In that way she could retain her power, hold on to the promise of her new single life in her two-bedroom apartment off South Street.

That position made me sad for the two of us, not just because it was such a familiar story but because I knew there had to be a secret side to it that I'd never get to the bottom of. Could Denise get to the bottom of it? Denise had brilliance and brains,

a drive to work into the earliest hours of the morning, a cha-
risma that was close to majestic. She wouldn't be destroyed by
any rejection letter. She wouldn't be restored by an acceptance
either. People are often afraid of what they want, and they'll do
anything in their power to make sure they don't get it, especially
when that object is just within reach. How many times in a life
do we fill out a form and decide not to carry its envelope to the
mailbox? But the allure of stopping scared the hell out of me. A
person could make a life out of those betrayals. The drive to do
yourself in was as strong as the drive of the world around you
to get the job done, whether it was from governments, schools,
or churches. Or maybe you were just mirroring their aggression, and you needed to do it yourself first in order to feel some
measure of control. I stopped laughing when Denise told the
rejection story a second and then a third time. I laughed out
of sympathy, but my laugh sounded less convincing with each
telling.

For all those reasons I decided to apply to Iowa. Not to compete with my friend, but because I needed to demystify risk, not
just for me but for her. There were practical steps in changing a
life. I *did* need to change my life, just as much as the speaker did
in the closing line of Rilke's "Archaic Torso of Apollo," though I
didn't doubt that more of it was out of my control than I could
ever know.

I got in. I felt dread. As I held that letter in my hands, I trem-
bled from my stomach down to my tight hamstrings, as if a draft
of cold air were falling through me. I moaned aloud: "And now
I have to go."

~~~~

I tried to convince myself Iowa City was another Creelman or Maidstone, one of the small, far-flung towns that Joni had grown up in. Not Saskatoon, which she'd moved to at eleven, but dusty, extreme, a place that organized time by the horn of the freight train. Its sky couldn't be ignored. It hovered above the grocery store, the gas station, and the primary school like an ocean turned upside down. It expressed itself at pressure points during the year—at *all* times of the year, but especially on the seams between seasons when it got humid and thunderclouds stacked themselves toward hot sun, or later in the year, when rain turned surfaces instantly to ice, making it impossible to use your front steps without falling flat on your back. It was why Joni said she'd come from "sky-oriented people" in "Paprika Plains." It was why the people cleared the dance floor in that song just to watch the rain come down. If you weren't a sky-oriented person, you'd likely get yourself in trouble in these parts. You had to align yourself with your senses; you had to distrust the forecast of a partly cloudy day when you saw those storm clouds on the horizon. It seemed far stranger, and more sublime, than my life in the Northeast, which struck me as too comfortable and routine, not challenging enough to stimulate my brain. Of course the ocean was far. It was farther than I had it in me to imagine (the Gulf at Galveston was 1,100 miles away), as were laughing gulls, the songs of redwing blackbirds, salt marshes, tides, sea breezes, waves thrashing bulkheads, waves pushing mats of bronze seaweed around, flagpole lines pinging against metal. I didn't have to look at water, but it meant everything to be near its motion, where the world felt activated, making itself up and tearing itself down all at the same time.

In truth, Iowa City was probably a more modest Saskatoon— flung out in the middle of the prairie but turned in on itself like a human inside a wool sweater. Built around a university, a river dividing it in two. I'd been in town for all of a week, coming to terms with the fact that I could barely see the sky from the window of my complex. The tree canopy softened things. The city, the east side in particular, reminded me of the older New Jersey: Collingswood and Haddonfield and Maplewood and Montclair. On some level I hadn't gone as far away as I'd pictured I would.

I'd figured out that the city stopped not far beyond the Sycamore Mall on the east side of town. A new concern: How would a person with such wanderlust carry himself in a place with such a constricted footprint? This would require imagination, but the imagination of a John the Baptist who knew how to occupy his mind when he wandered out into the desert. I had my classmates in the writers' workshop; I had the students in my rhetoric classes. There was Prairie Lights, the bookstore; the Hamburg Inn, a diner known for its pie shake, a dessert that was part soft-serve ice cream and part pie or sometimes cake. There were approximately 387 places to get smashed in Iowa City, and with an eye roll, one of my fellow students offhandedly said it had more bars per capita than any other place in America. Out in the town cemetery towered an eroded black angel, nine feet tall, atop a four-foot pedestal with heavy, weighted wings not so different from the crow costume Joni had worn on the cover of *Hejira*. It wasn't lost on me that that photo session took place in another Midwestern college town, on iced-over Lake Mendota at the University of Wisconsin–Madison, a little less than a three-hour drive away. The wings were about leaving the winter you once thought of as home. She had ice skates on. Was that an allusion to "River" and its long, frozen trail out of town?

If you were from the prairie, I could see why you'd leave. I could see why you'd crave Washington palms, freeways, jasmine, the golden sun, the breaking waves of Malibu, a spot on the earth where you didn't have to be pummeled by "the traitor cold," as she called it. I was told your eyelashes could freeze shut on the coldest days of winter, and I thought it was a joke until I breathed into the scarf around my mouth, and my eyelashes did exactly that on my walk to teach my rhetoric class in the basement of the campus's grimmest high-rise dorm. I found it electrifying and absolutely horrifying, two feelings I'd have to learn to hold simultaneously if I were to survive these two years.

~~~~

The truth was, I hadn't been thinking as pervasively about Joni as I had in years past. Something had happened to us. If this were another kind of relationship, this would be the point at which one of us would come in late at night and sleep on the living-room sofa rather than crawl under the covers of the bed we'd shared. Was I bored with her? Had I just metabolized her? Taken everything I needed from her and couldn't even see her as separate from myself anymore? There was an ugliness to that notion, the thought of using someone up and walking away, tossing them away like Kleenex, ashamed of myself, ashamed of her—so transactional, no gratitude.

The last time I'd seen her in concert was in 1983. My second Joni performance, in the same outdoor venue as my first. Philadelphia. Did I remember very much of it? The tour was in support of *Wild Things Run Fast*, an album I mostly loved, which didn't get the critical appreciation I thought it deserved. It was a return to pop, the pop of *Court and Spark*, after years of jazz experimentation: a couple of songs in the vein of 1960s' soul; one nodding to The Police in its rhythms; others talking back to the tossed-off, scrappy sound of early rock and roll, the music Joni had grown up dancing to in Saskatoon. But in live performances, Joni sounded less engaged with this new sound, though not for lack of trying. "Banquet" reimagined as a hard rock anthem, "Song for Sharon" with blocky, driving electric guitar chords. A quick, maybe obligatory appearance with the dulcimer on "A Case of You." I must have been excited about the setlist as I sat in those seats, but as soon as I left that venue? Gone. I didn't even know who came with me, who sat behind or in front of me, and I was a person who remembered everything, especially when I attached feelings, joyful or bleak, to an experience. When I looked at the VHS tape of the tour, picked up from a video store on a drive through Sarasota, I'd thought Joni wasn't at home in her phrasing. Her face looked impassive, cool, though there wasn't a second of the performance that was anything less than polished—the playing was tight. I found out later that she and her band had performed it on a soundstage, without an audience. Who was Joni without individual faces and bodies to sing to? Deafening applause between songs and ecstatic cries for more? Once, she recalled singing directly to the doe-eyed Prince in an aisle seat at one of her Minneapolis concerts, probably all of fifteen, before he was known to the world as Prince.

The late eighties didn't seem to know what to do with Joni, nor she with the late eighties. Time had made a misfit of her when, fifteen years before, she had stood at the center of it like she'd designed the clock. Whereas I had once listened to her every day, I now just as often listened to the Cocteau Twins, the Sugarcubes, Talking Heads, Talk Talk, Kate Bush. The grain of their music felt truer to an era of artifice and aspiration, and when Joni railed against decadence, as she did on *Dog Eat Dog* in 1985, she could sound hopelessly obvious. *We know this already*, I'd think. *You still have something to give, but not this. What about the best of you, conversational, wandering, questioning?* All this prophesying about the end of world. The sermonizing, the certainty in her voice— wasn't that Dylan's ground? Why couldn't the intimate and the political exist in the same song?

~~~~~

I'd never intended to break up with music. The thought of that would have sounded like sacrilege or, worse, self-destruction, but seismic change happened as it usually happens, not in an instant, like when it breaks apart an overpass during rush hour, but over years, as if it were done to me by an outside force, and I wasn't quite the instigator.

It happened like this: I stopped picking up my guitar as much as I used to. I passed the piano bench on the way to the bedroom, where I started giving myself over to novels with every free hour. Among those novels was Jane Bowles's *Two Serious Ladies*, which had once been assigned to me in a literature class and which I'd decided to reread outside of the duress of school. I didn't know what to make of its stunted, awkward sentences. Didn't know what to do with dialogue that struck me as artificial, stagey, though deliberately so. Was it making fun of Dickens? Was it an adult novel in the trappings of a children's book? Gradually I came to understand it as funny, painfully funny, broken in ways I couldn't quite articulate. Every character in it seemed to be crying for help, crying from the bottom of their souls, though doing what they could to mask that—and bumbling to the point of slapstick. It seemed to come from a mind that was as strange as Joni's, though it didn't sound like Joni. It sounded closer to punk, actually, if punk had been allowed to be vulnerable, soft, and ambiguous—it was the ambiguousness of emotion that got underneath my skin. When I put the book away, I obsessed over its odd characters, some bullied, some bullying, but all stranded in often underrepresented parts of the world, from Panama to Staten Island, where they were at odds with the local culture yet tried to make homes. It wasn't so much a story per se—after a couple of hundred pages, it just stopped, no resolution—but an extended dream on the page. Maybe that's what I'd been craving all along: representations of the world that reassured me that it was stranger than all the standard ways it had been interpreted. I was interested in anything that gave voice to people who didn't know how to speak about themselves or what they wanted but nevertheless tried to figure out ways to move forward.

I'd always loved words, but Joni had taught me to love them even more, as her high school creative writing teacher, Mr. Krantzman, had taught her. I'd wanted to be among people who valued making things, if only to feel less isolated. A part of me wondered whether the study of creative writing was a way to put off adulthood a little while longer—*adulthood* meaning a life that did everything possible to distract you from making things, which seemed central to what human beings were designed to do anyway.

As a teenager, I'd spent hours in my town library, a woody modernist building in the style of Frank Lloyd Wright, in which I pored over books of poetry: Charles Olson, Robert Creeley, May Swenson. They looked as modern as the building surrounding me. As modern as what Joni was trying to do, if *modern* is meant in its purest sense: pushing the parameters. I wasn't bothered that their books were written fifteen years back, ancient from where we were now, and were already looking sanctimonious and humor-free in the age of Donald Barthelme and Stanley Elkin, whose works drew energy from parody and collage. Their writing looked like music to me, and I felt its quaver off the page as I read it. I believed I'd found another source of animation aside from unexpected chords and dissonant words, and even if my poems failed, it didn't matter. I could bring what I'd learned to my lyrics.

I took a writing workshop the fall after graduating college. For class, I wrote a short story about a young boy named Red— Red for no other reason than I wanted a strong intense color to saturate the pages of the story. I'd set it in Naples, Florida, the first place after Southern California that I hadn't gotten carsick in on the family trips of my childhood. This meant that landscape was just as significant as the people in my story, though I didn't know this then. Landscape evoked the inner life. Red's mother, Natalie, who called him Plum, couldn't help making mistakes, often very public ones, as she was trying to bring them to a better life, away from her controlling father, Clem. She might have been having a mental health crisis, might have been struggling with an addiction to pills. The pressure was too much. Thus, at the end of "Patio Lights," she ended up making a snow angel in the grass of Naples, still wet from sprinklers, while Red and the rest of his neighbors looked on in the dark, afraid for her, afraid of their own confusion and shame and what it revealed about their weaknesses.

"Do you know what you did?" Barbara, my teacher, said one night after everyone else had gone home.

She was rushing me down the hallway of my old high school, where the class was held, her shoes beating the floor. I was hurrying to get away from her, as I hated hallways lined with lockers. I didn't want my life to change, at least not yet. It felt ludicrous that I'd taken myself back to the literal building that had both deadened and roused so much anxiety in me. Every time I looked at my yearbook photo, I couldn't help but be ashamed by what four years had done to me. My eyes flattened to the point of stupidity. Dead boy. Who had snuffed the light out of him?

If I'd been stronger, I would have known how to hide it, just like all my classmates had been hiding and using joy as their tool.

"Your story," she said. "It was beautiful. I didn't want that to go unsaid."

I nodded. She was glamorous in the way of a movie star, in a tight, tailored beige skirt, yet here she was, walking with me in everyday life. I felt grateful for her enthusiasm and told her so, blushing, but was confused as to why she'd held that back in class. Confused too to be praised. I didn't quite know how to handle it, in the same way I couldn't handle it from Albert years back. I'd seen people who didn't know how to accept compliments, and it made them appear uncaring, self-involved. It was never a flattering look. At the 1967 Newport Folk Festival, a fan's face went big when she found out she was facing Joni Mitchell. And Joni's response? She tore out of the festival grounds, on her feet, like a deer.

"Why did I do that, man?" Joni asked, shaken, to a friend who had watched her run.

There's no written record of an answer, but would Joni have been able to thank the fan or feel the heat of that fan's gratitude if she'd been able to hold what she'd already known? Fear of exposure, fear of commitment, fear of letting others down, of letting *herself* down. A nasty, number-driven music business in which women were especially disrespected in ways that were kept out of public view.

An ongoing issue, never resolved. For years she'd talked of running away from music in songs from "River" to "Taming the Tiger."

But didn't everyone want to run away? Everyone wanted to keep going forward so they couldn't be pinned down, couldn't be evaluated, mocked, and mourned. They wanted to keep changing shape; animals outsmarting their hunter.

I kept writing. I received awards from the state arts council. I went to Bread Loaf, where I served dinners and learned to chat about Jane Bowles with the famous writers in the dining room. I slid stories into envelopes, which produced a mildly narcotic effect, convincing me I was accomplishing a future. Life was telling me what it wanted from me. I still played the piano, still wrote songs, but unlike music, writing was sometimes harrowing for me. It took a full-body attention when it was a challenge to sit still, a condition that curled down into my neural pathways. The very thought of stillness made each bout of writing feel like a climb up a hill, as if a sentence had been issued from on high. Music never did that to me. It always took me to a place far away from the guitar or the piano, but now I no longer had the energy to mark up staff paper with quarter rests, which had once filled the hours. And if I did, it was merely to entertain and delight myself.

Writing didn't feel natural to me, but does writing ever feel that way to anyone? If it does, they're not trying hard enough. Language is unruly; language wants to mean ten things at once. That's exactly what I found compelling about it. By contending with a process that unnerved me, I was making sure it didn't dominate the person I tried to be. It was always steaming ahead of me, and it was my job to catch up.

The act of writing also made me think about the roles of my central characters, most of whom were witnesses rather than participants. They didn't make choices. They didn't defy or resist. My Bread Loaf workshop leader, Nancy Willard, quoted the words of another writer on my manuscript and wrote, "'Well, there are victims, and there are victims; let's take a look at yours.'" There was a kick inside that feedback, not just toward the story but in how I carried myself as a person. She caught me nodding at every word she said, trying to make her feel useful, appreciated. Following, spectating, reacting. A listener, a pleaser. Watching a mother flapping her arms in the wet grass.

But she was teaching me how to think and live, which is always greater than the sum of writing's parts. It took years to take in, metabolize.

I'd think of my stories as songs, long songs that needed to go all the way to the right margin. My songs needed a page rather than staff paper for now. That was where I'd begin, which is not to say I didn't at times think it was all a delusion.

I'd keep my musical life unlived as a way to protect it, so it could never be sullied, touched by the wrong hands, disparaged by the money system. The water of it would stay clean, so clean that I could slake my thirst with it for the rest of my days. I wasn't giving up, retreating in disappointment. I was taking care of music by protecting all the songs that would never get written. In *Missing Out*, psychotherapist Adam Phillips says our "unlived lives, our wished-for lives" are as significant if not more so than our "so-called lived lives."

~~~~~

But there was a third unexplored option: maybe that life didn't have to go unlived. Joni still thought of herself as a painter. She painted all of her album covers, had shows of her paintings in galleries. There was no question she took as much direction from Rembrandt, Gauguin, Matisse, and van Gogh as she did from Miles Davis. But the painter designation kept her from taking her music too seriously. By calling herself a painter, she could keep her music in the realm of play. She could give herself permission to say she'd give it up. Her identity didn't have to pivot on it. She tested out the sound of it in her mouth to see what it did to record industry executives' faces. ("This is going to be my last album." *"No!"*) In that way she could love music away from the obligation of business. She could keep some joy alive. As for her painting life? The art world was set up to dismiss it before it would even consider it, in the way it shrugged off the work of so many musicians who painted: Dylan, Kim Gordon, Don Van Vliet, David Bowie. Back then, unlike now, you only had one chance to do one thing well. No polymaths.

No musician-actor-fashion designer-dancer-graphic artist-record producer-influencer.

~~~~~

Occasionally Joni's name came up at a workshop party, and when it did, my ears pricked up like a retriever's. I'd be able to hear it from across the room, and I'd slide my way into a conversation in a way I wouldn't with any other subject, even literature. It was always a relief to say how much she meant to me, and I never knew how thirsty I'd been until I heard myself go on, and she went on ahead of me. Possibly I talked a little fast, my eyes glassy and elated, but I kept on going because the others seemed to enjoy it, this brand-new side of me, less private, brighter about my enthusiasms, willing to be so enthusiastic that I'd risk being an idiot in a culture in which we were always watching ourselves. But I didn't care if I was an idiot, just as I didn't care when Diana Ross's 1970 version of "Ain't No Mountain High Enough," almost twenty years after it had been a Top 10 hit, came on the stereo at a workshop party. I understood that it was more interested in the grandeur of one's emotions, in making a big statement of sound, than it was in evoking subtlety. Who cared if its orchestral treatment was right out of Harrah's Atlantic City? I didn't understand the common assumption that it was a joke and that it should only be listened to in secret, with the shades down. But someone in my workshop, a writer whom I'd admired deeply, caught me in my exuberance. I could see it in his face, a mixture of envy, tenderness, mild superiority, and horror that I'd allowed myself to let down my guard.

As to what we were expected to value across the arts?

Understatement. Control at all costs, even down to the level of the syllable. Nothing ornate or cadenced, too bright or too dark. High emotion, no. Was racism, misogyny, homophobia, classism twisted in its cloth? Likely. All of this was unsaid, of course. And if you crossed over an arbitrary line of expression, someone was always there to call you on it, which didn't mean he didn't want to cross over with you, because he knew that's where the life was. That's where growth and change were. But power didn't live on that side. Big agents didn't either. Contracts for first novels? No. So given the choice between life and death, some always chose death, with a knowing shake of a head and a rueful squint. They'd get to be in *The New Yorker* one day while you kept your beautiful life.

One day Joni's name came up with Martin, a poet from Canada, at Prairie Lights. I'd told him how much I loved her use of description. I talked about the farmhouse burning down, the twenty-nine skaters on Wollman Rink, the slick black cellophane of the palms, and he went silent, eyes a little helpless, worried. I couldn't tell whether his silence meant disapproval or whether he never thought any of her perceptions were rare enough to be re-marked upon. It took all of ten seconds to resume our conversation, but my sense was that I'd missed a major point about why poetry was serious and music was a different animal. But to have such a conversation would be joy-killing. He was a poet; I was studying fic-tion. Some lines weren't crossed, even though I'm not sure we knew what those lines were. It could have been as simple as intelligence versus stupidity. Sophistication and its opposite. We all stepped on the precipice of being impostors ten times a day.

Another day Joni came up with someone I knew a lot less but someone I was happy to get closer to—I wanted to know everyone, and the workshop was so large that it really was possible not to know some faces, especially if they kept to themselves and didn't show up for readings and parties. Claire talked at length about her favorite Joni songs, all of which came from *Court and Spark* and before, which was just fine. "'People's Parties'!" she cried, gesturing around us, as if Joni had actually written about the party at which we stood versus the one involving Apollonia van Ravenstein and Jack Nicholson. Her face went bright with the purest appreciation, a look I saw so little of when we are all punishing ourselves to be the best. Her complexion actually cleared. And how easily that appreciation slid into condemnation. Appreciation, condemnation—it was as if they'd always been siblings in the same house; they shared the same bedroom, the same bunk bed, and the trouble child had always been lying in wait, waiting to overshadow the good. She quoted from "Moon at the Window," a song I loved because it sounded like the route Joni might have taken if she'd run with the Charles Mingus influence. But it wasn't the music that made Claire complain. It was the lyrics and what they had to say about the moon: "At least . . . the thieves left that behind." "Could you think of anything more depressing?" she cried, laughing exuberantly as she said it, splashing her drink on her shirt and on the floor to give her point emphasis. That was it; that was everything that was wrong with Joni. She'd merely become a synonym for *depressing* when she'd already given us *Blue* and other exquisite portraits of despair.

Unfortunately, I didn't offer a countering opinion. I would have taken all of it personally if she wasn't already echoing a general idea that was common knowledge in the music press. The assumption was that Joni was a person who had squandered her art; her name was *a cautionary tale*. How could the person who wrote *Hejira*, *Don Juan's Reckless Daughter*, and *Mingus* put out the records that followed them? Records, with few exceptions, that seemed to cast aside anything she'd learned about her experiments in jazz. They bricked over the intricate chords that drew people to her music, whether they knew it or not. They fell into the trap of trying to please the music industry with possible hits. They were angry albums, angry about the environment and human greed and televangelists, but the anger felt like something else, aimed at targets off the page. In my less charitable moments, I thought of them as Gap ads painted by Picasso, which wasn't to say I didn't feel protective of them—the children of mine that incensed their teachers with their brash voices. I listened to them as much I did my favorite albums, with the faith that they'd show something to me that I didn't yet have the ears to hear.

Sometimes I'd write down the titles of the songs that pleased me the least—"Dancin' Clown," "Tax Free," "Shiny Toys," "The Reoccurring Dream," "Smokin'," "Ray's Dad's Cadillac"—then cross them out in self-disgust as if I'd dared to smite the holy one. It was interesting that two of these titles involved dropping *G*'s. Was that in itself a sign of fakery? That was it; she was faking. Faking like my classmates in high school with their overbright faces. Someone with sublime gifts was not allowed to fake, and when we caught her doing what we thought of as fakery, the punishment was especially severe. We thought she was the high priest of honesty and integrity on *all levels*, and now she was showing us what she was all along? Uh-uh. Not allowed. Betrayal. Out. Next victim.

And of course that Joni reference to bringing out boards, hammers, and nails—the crucifixion that awaits every too-beloved star of music—seemed less inflated, less narcissistic.

Did anyone else out there listen to Joni in their second-floor apartment on Governor Street? Maybe Joni embarrassed Martin for indulging too freely in all the things poets in the program were expected to transcend: autobiography, character, the bounds of personality, as if the goal had been always to speak from a more expansive place, a pasture of deep attention. So much less serious than the poets of ideas one was expected to aspire to: Tomaž Šalamun, Jorie Graham, John Ashbery, Derek Walcott. If Joni's work was energized by discipline, it wasn't the right kind of discipline. Joni cared about getting the lines straight, the colors right, burnishing and buffing every note until it satisfied *her*— first and foremost. Calibration. She believed in inhabiting every note as a way to defy erasure. By getting it right, she was giving birth to herself, on her terms rather than yours. She was saying *This is all mine* to a world that believed that art by a woman was lesser. Slight.

As far as the workshop, the point was *not* to be yourself, at least when it came to the narratives of one's life. To be a writer was to join a community, to take on its values. To dialogue with others who shared those values. To work from a position that implied I am different, I am an original? Not just audacious but naïve. There were too many writers who came before you, who shaped your thinking whether you appreciated that fact or not.

Much of that made sense to me. But if someone were to present this perspective to Joni, she'd probably say, *That's full of shit; don't be pretentious.* And anyone who thought like that was likely a man, who didn't know what it was like to move through the day as a woman or as someone Black, brown, queer, disabled. Someone who had taught herself to walk again.

~~~

Everyone described the program as competitive—it was key to its legacy. You didn't say yes to the acceptance letter without agreeing to the known: it was like signing on to med school or boot camp. There were stories of people who cried in workshop, and just as I'd thought one day, *No one cries in workshop—who made that one up?*, someone cried next to me, and it cut right through me even though it was aimed two feet away. The workshop leader in question kept digging into the blind spots in the story. His comments had a knife in them, and no one challenged him because they were afraid of retaliation and because he could make it seem that his feedback was no longer himself talking but *literature*, as if the terms of literature were as fixed and needle-straight as the Washington Monument. In the hallway after workshop, I stood by the door, waiting for the writer to come out. "That's such a good story," I said to her, quiet but cautious, so no one else would hear me. I didn't want it to get back to the leader. "Then why didn't you say anything?" she said, looking up at me. Because I was afraid? Because maybe if it were you, it wouldn't have to happen to me? Because I didn't want that narrative to wire my identity for the rest of my time in the program or maybe even for the rest of my life?

~~~

That was it; that was what bothered some about Joni—she had stopped caring. Or seemed to. She'd had it with the music industry. "Dancin' Clown." Was it a joke on the business, all the parts of its machinery? I believed she had it in her, that Joni, in the manner of her mooning the listener on the cover of her *Misses* compilation. To make the machine happy, she'd lubricated *Chalk Mark in a Rain Storm* with celebrity appearances, everyone from Billy Idol to Wendy & Lisa to Tom Petty to Willie Nelson. You couldn't even listen to a song on it without a celebrity appearance in the fore or background, and maybe that made it harder to deride, maybe that made it sound current, hip, which was what some said it wasn't in the time of "West End Girls," "Papa Don't Preach," and "Smooth Operator." I suppose that *was* depressing, as if the person who'd always been above the concerns of popularity was playing into them, along with them. Half-cynical but not wholly, which in truth might have been the darker way to turn.

~~~~~

The days were moving faster than I could process. All the readings, all the parties and the dinners—the social aspect was like being overstimulated for days on end but without the amphetamines. I was running all the time, sometimes literally, out of breath. What was it doing to my writing, which was coming more slowly now that I was investing too much in coherence, consistency? How close I was to being exposed for my hubris, my inexperience. Just like with Martin—one false note. I'd gone there: maybe? And what few tools I had at my disposal to cover that up. Covering it up: that struck me as a tool to cultivate if one was going to thrive in this environment. It didn't have to be like this, but it was a function of the culture. My hunch was that most of my fellow writers had grown up being told they were smart, and they were expected to live up to that assessment. They'd gone to prestigious colleges, prep and boarding schools, whereas I'd gone to Rutgers, with its egalitarian spirit. They'd been listened to. Aced standardized tests. Grown up thinking they had the right to speak and believed their words were significant, even when they hadn't read the assignment. "Did you read the assignment?" asked Sean before our craft class one day, seconds before our teacher walked into the room. "No," we all mumbled in unison, looking down at the handout, ashamed. He hadn't either, he admitted. And after our professor was settled at the head of the table and asked us a question about the use of description in the ending, Sean threw out such an impeccable answer in which all the clauses lined up with such conviction, it was as if he'd confessed to us simply to impress us: his high-wire act between the trees of Davenport Street. Had he actually read it? I didn't think so, which was sadder and more cynical than if he'd lied to us. Where was curiosity? And soon it didn't even matter, as our professor, a guest writer who was on the verge of massive attention, spoke with messianic zeal about the story at hand, and we'd all rather hear his voice than our own, as his always came with a deep belief in the power of literature, whether he was talking about the class struggles in Isaac Babel or in Alice Munro. Maybe that's what we wanted for ourselves: his raw belief that literature could change lives, which had always felt more significant than any paragraph we'd ever tried to pin down.

Over the course of the semester, Sean stopped trying to impress. He, along with others, went silent, but that didn't stop our professor from asking the most pressing questions. The questions would be followed by silence, the usual uncomfortable space. A skirt shifting in a chair, chalk dragging across the blackboard until it cracked in half. We learned to be uncomfortable in that pot together, person to person, sitting inside our shame, our salty soup. We attempted to look thoughtful, pretending to be thinking about time, illness, and death when we were also wondering when the liquor store closed or how many weeks were left in this unending semester.

But that didn't mean that I wouldn't return to this moment in thought at another point when I was calmer, better to take it in. I was still talking back to that question about Alice Munro twenty years later.

~~~~

To get away one day, I drove out to the country. I'd been feeling the end of town like the end of a room, the waiting room of a doctor's office, and I had to get away. I had to be under some sky, which was part of the reason I had come: I could bear grad school if I could take in the sky, the prairie unfurling to infinity, a barn and grain elevator stippling the horizon. The openness of it always put me in a calming trance, which was just the correction I needed after the scratch of human voices, spoken and on the page. I drew closer to a set of buildings, a Quonset hut, a ribbed silo. It couldn't be. A pig as big as a school bus, black with oblong white patterns, chowing down on some corn and tossing grains around. I pressed the brake as close to the floor as I could, hypnotized, questioning. The road behind me was empty. I was fully aware I could be inventing this pig just as much as I'd been inventing my sequence of stories about Red and his mother over the past year and a half. I wouldn't tell anyone, not even my closest friends, as

I could already picture the concern and the doubt on their faces. I'd keep the pig totally to myself. My postcard charm. I broke out in laughter, big piggy joy.

~~~~

That chord, so warm, so near. The ache inside its voicing, the blend of tension and slackness in the strings. I leaned in again and recognized it beneath the everyday supermarket noise. "That Song About The Midway." Joni. A voice that had once been so close, and now I had to strain to identify it? I looked down into my shopping cart, filled with ramen and powdered soup mixes and red wine I hadn't cared enough to want. What would I let go of next? She'd given me so much. I left the cart by the glass doors of frozen dinners and walked straight out of Econofoods.

~~~~

I was back home for winter break when I had the strange sensation to take myself to the living room. I had spent my childhood looking out the window of that living room, awaiting the mail truck, and here I'd put myself in that same position. Back then I believed I was jinxing good fortune to stare at the mailbox too hard. Somehow I believed I wouldn't get the mail I'd been hoping for if I tried to will it. The trick was to pretend to be interested in anything but the object of desire, and lift my head *only* after I heard the truck pass to the Spadeas' yard. By that time I'd refined my hearing enough to know exactly what the motor sounded like, all its gradations of low notes, a vaporizer with a head cold. I'd developed the sensitivity of a black Lab waiting for his human's car after spending all day by himself.

The envelope was addressed from the agency from which I'd applied for the award. My breathing slowed, and a hormone probably spiked. I couldn't take it. It was best to prepare myself for disappointment in regard to anything related to wanting and art. I'd learned that back in my teenage years, when I was writing music. To be an artist at any stage is to deal with rejection, rejection, wait-lists, and even positive rejection, scribbled with hasty notes—*Try us again!*—and I was thinking about the luck and arbitrariness of it all. *Nobody who's good gets awards anyway*, I thought as I looked down to read I'd won a fellowship for twenty thousand dollars.

I can't recall how I told my parents or Denise—all of it was clouded by the destabilizing force of exultation, which is not without its pains. It takes you somewhere to the realm of wordlessness. It reduces you to an animal, to your senses, and you feel as confused as if you've been given a great meal after a time of deprivation and you might never eat again. This is it. Your last chance—behold! Though I do remember the look on my parents' face, a kind of satisfaction, which looked like their souls had relaxed after years of being worried about me, my outcome. I loved them so much. They weren't like Joni's mother, whose mixed feelings about her daughter's life as a musician refused to settle. For that I felt grateful to them, and even though I didn't say it, I let it shine through my eyes. They could relax for now—or for the next six months. I saw their shoulders falling back, their chins lift, their faces brighten.

"You always wanted to be famous," said my father, grinning like a kid.

It was something that he said in appreciation from time to time, every time something good happened to me. Without fail, it made me feel exposed. And when had I said this? When I was four? Five? It misunderstood something about what I wanted to do with my work, though if you'd asked me what I wanted to do, I'm not sure I could have said it. Fame was tawdry, cheap. Fame was the kind of thing that had sent Joni running from the folk festival because she hadn't wanted to be harvested. She wanted something deeper and more ineffable that had little to do with herself but something outside her, something she couldn't see and didn't even want to. Why else keep reaching?

But maybe fame was what my father had always wanted. For him it was to be loved, for someone to smile on a face that wasn't used to benevolence directed its way.

When I came back to the workshop, all the spotlights were on me. Some had applied for the award and were rejected; they'd seen the announcement, and word had spread. I tried not look at people to see if they knew, and inevitably I looked at their faces as if I were seeking them out, hungry. Abigail, always cool and indifferent to those outside her inner circle, talked to me for the first time, her eyes dark, complexion white, black hair gorgeous, shining. "Congratulations"—but said in such a way that it felt flat, that it said, *You changed the equation for us. Now we have to go out and get that award?* As if big advances, literary-agent-of-all-literary-agents Binky Urban's representation, and publications in *The New Yorker* and *The Atlantic* weren't enough? Jesus.

Or maybe that was just me. It had to be me. Everybody was happy for me.

I was pulled into the community in a way I hadn't been pulled into it before. I was assigned a role. The role came with expectations, assumptions. You think it's exactly what you've wanted all along, but you're expected to live up to a position in which the requirements are ever shifting and unnamed. The director of the program not only fixed his eyes on me but actually said my name when I stepped into a party, and the room quieted a bit; ears turned before the din came back. I felt hunted. And what that meant was that I couldn't put up half-baked work in workshop anymore. I had to put up distinguished work, whatever that meant, and I was at a point where I didn't even know what I was doing. I wanted to be better, braver, wilder, more. With every word I laid down, I heard Jasper saying, "Him? Why him? Why shouldn't that have been me?" So I deleted the sentence as soon as I typed it out. I lay down another, swallowed against my sore throat, and deleted it again.

In order to be extraordinary, you have to be a little bad first. You have to be mediocre until you're able to say, *I don't want to wear this coat; I don't have to. I can wear brilliant colors if I want to. I have my sights on the sky, the clouds.*

I couldn't make what I needed to make, and here I was, stuck with this coat, some too-long vintage piece of crap, dusty, with missing buttons, something I'd picked up from Ragstock, one of the vintage stores in town.

I got a little crazy, but not in any of the conventional, external ways. I kept the thunderstorm inside my head, and no one knew, even the people who were my friends. The assumption was that agents and editors were leaving messages on my phone—they weren't. This became one more thing to hide, and my thunderstorm grew wilder.

～～

The workshop prom was a frenzy. Part of it was the absurdity of the concept, the bald idiocy of the word, but it was tradition, and we were all too eager to let loose after the ongoing stress we'd been through. The night fell at the end of the year, just after we'd wrapped up our final classes. A lot of drink, and what relief to be set free from the constraints of the classroom, all that convention and pressure. Two years together. People who hadn't looked one another in the face all year did so with warmth, affection, and sadness over anticipated departures. The gay and lesbian people—all three of us out of a hundred (*three?!*)—were laughing like we hadn't laughed before. What a relief it was to dance together, all of us, as a group. Why hadn't we done more of it together instead of confining it to the floor of the 620, the gay bar across Burlington Street, as if dancing were something peripheral to our lives, dark and louche, dangerous, something you wouldn't want to be caught doing, especially if you were a straight person? The more we kept dancing, the more I started rising out of myself, rising out of what I had kept down in myself as a gay person, and I didn't know what had gotten into me—I wasn't drinking, or at least not that much. I got much higher from dancing for an hour, without a break, than I had ever got from beer or wine, but I climbed the seven steps to the stage and started dancing, up there in front of the crowd. I was dancing higher than anyone else in that room. I didn't think I might have looked ridiculous. I wasn't imagining that some of my gestures might have been scrutinized or recorded. I wasn't exactly in the world that was laid out before me, and maybe that's why I jumped from the stage, all six feet of it, landed on my feet, and kept on dancing in spite of the ache in my ankles and heels. It didn't occur to me that I should feel pain, and so I didn't. I didn't crash into anyone's arms, as there weren't any arms to crash into—not then or any time soon. And maybe that's what gave wing to my flight. I needed to be higher than everyone else for just this once in order to come back down to earth.

~~~~

And on the day of our departure, my friend Katrina and I held on to each other as if we were trying to hold our bodies in place. And maybe Joni's musical restlessness was a way to make sure she wasn't going to let that happen to her, as much as she might have wanted it to. How could anyone pin you down and say what was good when you took away their markers, their lines, their syntax, their structure? When you stretched out the grid so far across that the squares went lopsided and you turned it into a spiderweb? How could anyone fire a gun at you if you kept on changing form, kept outsmarting them—even those whom you believed were on your side? There you were, coyote to wolf to deer.

BLACK CROW

〜〜〜

IN FRONT OF THE UNITARIAN UNIVERSALIST MEETING HOUSE IN Provincetown, Manuel asked me if the rumor he'd heard going around town was true: Was I seeing the poet? I'd told him yes, I was. I felt uncharacteristically complicated about telling him the truth, alternately shy and proud. And before I could fill him in on the unexpected transition of our relationship from friendship to the romantic, he'd said, "He's really big."

I laughed, more out of nervousness and surprise than anything. Big, of course, meant accolades: the National Poetry Series, the National Book Critics Circle Award, the Los Angeles Times Book Prize, Britain's T. S. Eliot Prize, all of which he'd received for his third book, his breakthrough. Admirers included James Merrill and W. S. Merwin. But for Manuel, big meant something larger, undefined, unbounded, greater than a single human body. It meant a force akin to magic, a distillation of what people craved, a cloud twisting through the branches above us, shapeshifting, sparrows whipping through it. There was something gorgeous about big. Something intimidating too about how proximity to it could make you lose yourself.

The news of us was all of two weeks old, if that. It was 1995, a few days into April, when on a warm day, you could go outside without your winter coat. In Provincetown you could sneeze in the east end, and it would be reported back to you by the time you walked all three miles to the breakwater, sometimes as a head cold, occasionally as pneumonia.

I leaned into his reaction in terms of what it meant for the two of us, our casual friendship. He was a poet too, and poets, more than any other humans, are attuned to grades of change in interpersonal weather. He looked at me as if a relationship with a famous person changed the mathematics of everything, right down to what you ordered for lunch.

In spite of Manuel's excitement, bigness was against what Provincetown stood for—officially. Provincetown, in the words of my artist friends, made up its own rules. Provincetown thought it was high above them, especially when it came to writing and the making of visual art. It was part of why I'd been drawn to the Fine Arts Work Center in the first place, why I'd accepted the fellowship once I'd applied for it after Iowa. It was why I'd stayed on in town after my two years of a stipend and housing had come to an end. In no time at all, I'd made a religion out of Provincetown. If Laura Nyro, Grace Paley, and Frank O'Hara could make a religion out of New York City, then maybe I could do that with the catwalk of Commercial Street, the cold mineral funk of the harbor. The religion, as I tried and failed to live it, was fed by two streams, in harmony and opposed. The first one was the community, involving oneself in it. To be a participant was to look out for people, listen to them, take time to see how they were doing when you ran into them on the street. It meant to look beyond the one or two people you depended upon. You always had more room inside of you than you thought you did, and if you weren't overwhelmed by what that asked of you, you could keep expanding yourself until maybe you were less yourself as a single entity but multiple: someone who figured in the lives of many people and who was thus a different person for each of them.

The religion meant cultivating your idiosyncrasy: your eye, your ear, the lifts and turns of your speech patterns. It meant bringing those characteristics to your work, which might mean giving yourself the permission to write the kind of thing that only a small set of people might take the time to comprehend and love. Should that be a matter of shame? It sounded like a dynamic life to me, but when I thought back to my MFA classmates, I couldn't imagine many of them would have agreed. At least one of them had said that if she wasn't going to be published by Alfred A. Knopf within two years after grad school, she was applying to law school, where the reward for achievement was a freeway with marked exits.

~~~~~

But on the other hand, bigness required you to let go of something scarier than I had a grasp of: the fiction of your control.

From the perspective of my closest Provincetown friends, big-ness was against the do-it-yourself. It was a watered-down cocktail. Bigness was in sync with the system. It oiled the machinery of numbers, markers, and money. But on a gut level, that made it sound simpler than it actually was. The truth was, you probably couldn't control bigness when it came looking for you. It was the crow that hovered just above you for years, and just when you thought you'd come to terms with the incessant beating of its wings, it tapped its feet gently on your head before bearing you up. And to be a part of bigness was to be in submission to it, though it looked to everyone else like you were in charge. And you couldn't talk about how it scared you to be up there, abiding all those eyes for twenty minutes. No one wanted to hear about that—it was lazy, ungrateful. "Teeth sunk in the hand," as Joni sang. You had everything every other artist wanted to have, so you endured it for that reason. And there you were, speeding from a delayed plane to a bookstore when your travel schedule was such that you'd had nothing to eat all day but a cup of coffee, a spoonful of orange preserves, and a roll with a pat of icy butter.

When we said goodbye, Manuel already felt a little further from me, uncertain he'd had the right to hug me anymore. I'd already slipped into another space for him, more dream state than real. *Don't do that*, I thought, the words so close to the tip of my tongue. *Please.*

And then I said it: "I'm not that person. Stick a knife in my side if I ever am."

On some days I was learning more than I cared to learn.

~~~~~

The blue hutch of my new dining room was filled with CDs by artists I only peripherally listened to: Handel, Natalie Merchant, Des'ree, Annie Lennox, Aretha Franklin, Billie Holiday. Maybe living with someone else's music, whether in the house or on long drives off Cape, called me back to Joni, my sonic foundation, a music about which I could say: mine. *Turbulent Indigo* had come out the year before, and Joni was talked about, written about, and played again in public in ways she hadn't been in years. She was back, the media proclaimed, as if she'd been in hiding on a French mountaintop for the last fifteen years. I listened to that album so many times that I'd overhear my friends humming scraps of "The Sire of Sorrow" and feel a thread of mischievous satisfaction knowing that the song had reached them indirectly through me.

Which called me back to her previous work. In the midst of finding my footing in my new life, I was once again scouting down everything I could find out about Joni, including a film of her 1974 performance in London. Or, more specifically, a piece of it in the library basement.

She isn't the same Joni of the *Miles of Aisles* recording. In *Miles of Aisles*, she tells rambling stories between songs; she sounds playful, on the edge of a joke. She laughs at an audience member's spontaneous outburst: "Joni, you have more class than Richard Nixon, Mick Jagger, and Gomer Pyle combined." And she enjoys playing a range of selves: the vulnerable folk singer; the sleek, budding jazz singer, mimicking a Bugs Bunny voice for laughs at the piano. There's none of that in the London performance, even though it's a stop on the same tour, in support of *Court and Spark*. Listening to *Miles of Aisles*, you could trick yourself into thinking she'd come into what she'd longed for as an artist. Popular success, if it's to be measured by chart positions, is happiness. She isn't the depressed, and reportedly sick, person trying to stay alive from minute to minute back when she was recording *Blue*.

What's unnerving about the London performance is how little Joni opens her eyes. When she does, she's invariably looking up toward the rafters and not at the audience. And her expression isn't collected, but, what—haunted? Unsettled? Bewildered? Of course, she is performing the role with all the finesse of an actor, but she isn't spinning this role out of the air. At one of the few points she addresses the audience, she talks about only seeing the first rows—beyond that it must be dark—and in those rows, she sees about twenty movie cameras. Periscopes, she calls them. "Sneaky," she says, with a laugh, but there's ice behind the laugh. Later, when people are shouting out unintelligible phrases and wishes, she starts banging some high notes on the keyboard with steely consternation: a schoolteacher from the Alberta prairie. The stage light manager, in a comment on the YouTube video of this concert, explains that she'd had a cold that night, but there's no way you can hear that from the quality of her vocals, which are always clear, every note inhabited. She *willed* that.

Only when she's close to the end of the concert does her face warm up. She can see that her ending is near, and she can put to sleep this selling of herself until the next night.

~~~~~

I prided myself in being able to tell the difference between three and four a.m. light in the bedroom. Though it was dark, it wasn't *dark* dark, the window square a haunted deep blue behind the rime of ice. To be attuned to those gradations I had to be a little bit of an animal, but I also had to sync them up with a clock that could be as elusive as standard tuning.

He was sleeping, sleeping deeply. Half snore and a little cry. I knew he was supposed to be up at four thirty. I knew it wasn't my duty to be the caretaker of his schedule, and in truth, he never expected that of me. He did not need a parent.

Still, I turned my face to the clock on the nightstand: five thirty a.m. One hour *after* he was supposed to get up and fly to San Francisco.

A shaking of his forearm. The alarm. It never went off?

A curse, a leap out of bed, the shower turning on. Sink running. Banging. Hearts banging. Closet door. Out the window, the taxi was waiting by the fence, engine on, headlights on. Windshield wipers. The driver didn't care—probably. It was probably nice to get some rest, to close his eyes and be lulled to half sleep by the latest Celine Dion on the radio.

And so began the life of endless motion, of being side by side with a traveling writer who wanted to walk, run, and fly through space as much as he wanted to be still.

What would happen if he missed his connection at Logan? I didn't say it, but that's what I'd really wanted. He wanted it too, at least today after he'd been visiting colleges for weeks. After he'd write an email apologizing for travel troubles to the host, we'd head out for breakfast, and the day that started out in turbulence would go calm, a little like a snow day but with open roads. Omelets at the breakfast place out on Shank Painter. A walk with the dogs out on the fire road by Hatches Harbor. Maybe he'd go back to his study and work on a poem. Maybe I'd head over to my desk and take notes on my next chapter. And we'd be together for a little while, as if our lives were fully contained within the walls of our eighteenth-century house or, at most, the borders of our town. The town would feel less isolated than it often did off-season, and we could again be in awe of the place in the manner of a new arrival. The amber light of winter. Stripped trees. The waves in the distance, out in Herring Cove, which roared over parts of town like a jet engine on the runway at Logan.

But he was off again. Made the cab, made the tiny plane by ten minutes, just before they shut the door. And so went the project of filling up the rest of the day with projects, the feeding of the two dogs, the reading of eight low-residency manuscripts. A self-constructed schedule to stanch my loneliness.

Did I even say how much I loved him, loved our life together? I loved walking down the street with him, loved working in the garden together. I loved our camaraderie, which felt like a mysterious presence of its own, a third person. Did we have much in common? Other than a shared interest in literature, maybe not, but when we did find something we were both crazy about—say, Elizabeth Bishop or Laura Nyro's *New York Tendaberry* and *Gonna Take a Miracle* albums—we loved it entirely, our mutual enthusiasm running like a flood. Mostly I think we saw characteristics in each other that we didn't possess in ourselves, and believed in something that was more felt than stated: an exchange of preternatural materials. The change of us happened sporadically, over months, and then we were in it together, living together. I'd never given myself the time to ask, *Is this what I want of my life?* because that was not how an artist lived. When adventure came calling for you, you gave it your full yes, even if you were scared, even if you knew you were about to leave so much of your past lives behind. The odd thing about being an adult is how fast your life can change. Faster, certainly, than childhood, which seems to last two thousand years, with puberty smack in the center of it. One day you're dancing yourself sweaty for two-and-a-half hours straight in a nightclub by the harbor, and the next you're sitting on a sofa atop an old rug with roses and a sky-blue border, in a living room overheated by a fireplace, two retrievers asleep by your feet. Without knowing it, you have less in common with your old friends, with their lack of ties to people, houses, objects. You talk to them a little less because you don't know what to do with the stops and starts in your conversations. You say *wisteria*, but it is heard as *Washington*, and you can't seem to get your voices back in sync.

The two of us used the word *partner* long before my old friends were remotely comfortable with it.

~~~~

And sometimes, when our schedules aligned, I came along on his travels.

Invariably I sat in the front row, in a prominent position, beside him. We always talked together beforehand, gave enthusiastic hellos to whomever came up to talk to us, and when the introducer read their words, I concentrated on every word, as if to make sure the introducer knew that they were being attended to and appreciated. I got used to performing being watched without being too self-conscious about it. The trick was not to look too involved but to listen, genuinely listen. And by that I mean I don't believe anything about that role was inauthentic. I loved his work, loved hearing how he shaped each line, shadowed certain words, how he organized the reading, which differed from night to night, as if he were teaching me something profound about structure, about how structure *is* thinking, for who else but me would know that he was shuffling things around, making fresh conversations from night after night? He made no secret of the fact that Chet Baker was one of his idols, and that showed in his delivery. It was a love letter in sound, but only I knew that. And it helped that the work came out of our life together, even though our life was only occasionally the subject of the poems.

But some of the poems *did* feature a version of me. Or, more accurately, ideas that had begun with one of my gestures or reactions. Sometimes my name appeared. Or my face of calm when we were told our plane's stabilizer had malfunctioned, and now was the time to put your head down in your lap and prepare for an emergency landing.

In such situations the room was all eyes. I felt them darting, even if they were pretending to look ahead.

So he wasn't ever the only one onstage, though that was not officially so. Afterward someone inevitably said, "I loved watching your eyes, the reaction on your face." I was a part of the performance, which was about love, really, and loving well, over the long term, in the wake of devastating loss. My face said that love didn't stop with the death of his partner, who had been gone two years now, but that it kept going on, not just for himself but for the people in the room, all the way to the back of the hall, and beyond.

But tonight it became complex in the signing line, as it sometimes did. So many people—twenty deep? Thirty? Out through the auditorium door, snaking out into the hall, and the line never moved quickly, no. Everyone was attended to, and if you wanted to stand in that line, you'd better be generous about that. People had lost so much, and when someone lost somebody to AIDS—they lost on multiple levels: their relationship to neighbors, their ties to relatives who had refused to comprehend their grief—you had to take it seriously. What those relatives didn't say? *Well, what do you expect? He was gay.* Meaning that he could have stopped being gay, as one could stop smoking, drinking, gambling, snorting coke. *He didn't always use condoms.* And they didn't know, maybe until many years later, what such responses revealed about themselves. As if there should be a grief limit depending on the supposed moral stature of the mourned one.

Some writers write work that makes readers want to walk out and gather themselves immediately afterward. It is all too intense, private, and they're not sure how they even feel about the work until a day has passed, and maybe then they're still puzzled. But my partner? His work made people want to come up to him and hold him. They saw themselves in him. He spoke their anguish, their wish to love the world again in all its minutiae in the midst of their own desolation. And in that way he shared Joni's wish to connect.

But then there were people who wanted too much of him, who tore into his time with their experience. The fine line between fandom and narcissism—some didn't care that there might be twenty people behind them, patient, weary, worrying about somebody at home. And at such points, I thought, *How do I hold myself? Where do I place myself in the room—close beside that pillar, or at some distance?* I stood several feet in the dark, hands behind my back, looking on with benevolence, trying to make sure my features didn't harden. There was something about my face, its hard lines and edges. The thinking in it could so easily be mistaken for anger.

And always at the back of my mind, Peter Doyle stands on a grassy hill at Camden's Harleigh Cemetery as Walt Whitman, his former lover, is buried in the glen below. The police guarding the funeral almost turning him away after Whitman's closest friends had wanted him out of there.

"You're so lucky," said a man who caught me off guard, which seemed to be the intention.

It was true. I *was* lucky. I felt that at every moment in the manner of someone who wasn't entirely down deep in his life. You couldn't do it otherwise. But the voice behind those words sounded part benevolent, part aggressive—it was impossible to tell the two apart. He knew there was nothing for me to say but one thing: "You're right." He didn't know that he wasn't exactly talking about me. Rather, he was talking about my partner. The man wasn't allowing him to be a fallible human being, which wasn't fair to him, who was expected to be a prophet, if not Buddha or Jesus Christ. The man didn't hear the reproach embedded in his words. *One false move and you'll be called on it. We'll be disappointed. We'll walk away from you.*

It never occurred to me to leave the room; walk through the glass doors, down the steps, down the walk; watch birds over-head; walk down to a patch of water and think about what was making those expanding rings in the murk. Those suds. To let go of what—control? The human conundrum—control. Yes, I was watching him for myself, but he also needed me to see that he was doing well—it was *my* seeing above all that mattered. His work needed a witness. I was its recording. The people in line? The people in line were thinking about themselves, their own relationships and losses, which is the way it was always supposed to be. The work my partner wrote was a portal. Once his readers stepped into the house of the work, all his individual markers slipped away, and they were inside their senses, their bodies, the towns and cities in which they'd grown up. Their houses. A new front room, stairwell by the door, sun coming in through the skylight, warming a lopsided rectangle on the floor. The stairwell they'd been looking for for years but needed some help when it came to finding it, climbing it.

~~~~~

I looked down at the page. I looked out the window. Once I came up with a sentence that I liked enough, I looked out the window some more, as if by staring, it would happen all over again. But this practice let in so many thoughts and sensations that I didn't know how to shape them, what to put on the page, what to leave off. My brain felt like a rubber band pulled to its extreme, then snapping back to its original shape, a little looser each time. I was floating above my chair now. Fifteen minutes. A fire siren outside? Barking retriever? Only an external perception pulled me into myself. Until I stretched myself out again and repeated the whole procedure.

Was I making a mess? To bear with the possibility of failure as long as I could stand it, to make friends with it so the dread no longer felt like someone I wanted to push out the back seat but someone I could learn from if I cultivated patience. Two words that sounded like abrasion at first but were the beginning of energy.

I was writing a novel about a seventeen-year-old narrator who moves in with an older man in his Coral Gables, Florida, neighborhood. Eventually he leaves that man and helps his brother fix up and remodel a run-down motel on the other side of the state, by the Everglades, near Naples. It was a book about plants and weather as much as it was about the characters. In fact, its setting *was* a character, an embodiment of the collision of artifice and the natural world and all the ways humans were using that landscape to their own ends. But no novel works without a voice, and Evan was the best narrator out of the four initial voices—always I started big before winnowing down. The struggle was how to write a book with a gay teenage narrator, represent his experience without neutering him, and reach a larger band of readers. It was as important to me that the book find its way into the hands of a young man struggling to understand his sexuality as it was the hands of a thirty-six-year-old mother of two who was interested in reading a novel set in Southwest Florida. That didn't strike me as unreasonable, that reach. I wanted it to touch everyone in the largest sense. And besides, who didn't intuit connections between the body and all its mysteries and the burgeoning of trees, marsh, vines?

I knew there were more efficient ways to go about writing a book, but I couldn't do it unless I was discovering something unexpected with each line. That was the thing that kept the engine going, not a premeditated plan of action, outwardly turned. And this was why some asked the writer the cringe-making question: What is your process? It came from the belief that the writer had the secret. If only you did this one trick, you'd get it right. Because no one wanted to tether themselves to a chair for three hours at a time and conjure up a mere two sentences. You didn't want to wake up to a paragraph that looked inflated and imprecise when its arrangement had seemed auspicious the night before.

And no wonder that, when given the choice between filling out a tax form and writing, some writers would put off writing in order to do the tax form. Because a tax form had sequential steps. It gave you the sense that you were doing a good job. Finishing it gave you a sense of satisfaction and, on top of that, the illusion of more time, time to do what you'd wanted to do . . . your writing.

My benchmark was higher now that some were paying attention. It was one thing to develop as an artist on my own—quite another to do so when the spotlight was following me around, when some were holding my work in comparison to the one I loved. I had no room to fail, which felt a little like winning that fellowship back in grad school, but the pressure was ten times larger. And it wasn't simply to be "good," whatever that meant. I'd wanted to give to others what Joni had given to me, which was more than a sequence of brilliant albums. Her work had given me a chart as to how one lives a life, evolving over time, rejecting a previous self, trying out a self simply through a new palette of tunings, keys, instruments, and washes of sound. It was the truer way to think about time, implying that progress was never in line with the calendar or the clock; it was never linear. The body of her work was the body of a landscape: here a bombing range, there a plateau. And you couldn't think about the work as a whole unless you were thinking about how each part talked back to the entire landscape.

Of course I could give into the pressure, but, no—I wasn't going to stop, no. Occasionally I was summoned by the allure of that and knew that turning my back on my work would kill me. Given the choice between a relationship and art? There was no doubt of my answer. What else was there to do when you didn't write? Eat, mate, masturbate, pay your bills, exercise? I was haunted by the partners of famous gay poets who had entertained ambitions to be writers in their own right and somehow retreated, stood back in the shadows, numbing the pain of that with jug wine or afternoons in front of *Days of our Lives* on full blast. As if to function as a muse couldn't coexist with being an independent artist. One role assigned to each in a life, and that was your drinking stream.

I couldn't write without bringing in the sound of the house, the sound of our life together: the walking of the dogs, the trips to the hardware store and the gym. But how to do that without sounding like my partner? If I'd been a different kind of writer, I could have written something that shaped itself so far away from him that I'd keep a wide territory between us, like we were two separate bedrooms in different wings of the house. But I didn't want to divide the world into two. My own work was often suspicious of binaries; it was about wanting to challenge or dissolve them. I didn't want to simply write *against*, a counterculture. I wanted a third option, in-betweenness. And yet whatever decision I made on the page felt like it was talking back to his work, and there was no way I could get around that.

I wanted to write of love, but I also wanted to write about the darker sides of human nature. I didn't want to be afraid of thinking about cruelty and indifference, someone loving someone so much that they walked away from them at the restaurant and didn't call back for days, if at all. What was love if I couldn't find the filaments of darkness inside it? I wanted all the mixed-up colors in between. Not here and there but all at once, simultaneous. And maybe that was one way to touch a reader's nerves. And maybe that was one way to carry my work to the other side of the river.

Every time I spread darkness on the page, the darkness was all the editor seemed to fix upon. When my first novel went out on submission, an editor wrote as part of a rejection letter: "This past summer I met Paul and his partner at a reading in Provincetown. When I came to this novel, I was expecting Paul to be a good person, but the character that I encountered on the page disappointed me."

And this was why he'd said no: a flash of mind he hadn't expected to see, hadn't wanted to see. Had he known how much this would ache? A little cut taken out of the soul, but that was exactly what he had in mind.

I was supposed to be good, at all times.

Do you know how to make someone go a little crazy, be a little mean, or worse? Tell them they have to be good at all times. Tell them all eyes are on them, waiting for them to slip.

All eyes were on me. Well, not really, that is an exaggeration, but it felt like that every time I sat down at my desk. My work ended up being a little meaner than I actually was, just to say, *No, you won't do that to me. You won't put me in that box.*

Sometimes writing about love doesn't look like love.

In the end I published *Lawnboy* with a wonderful small press after my agent came close to selling it to two trade houses. It sold so many copies in its first month, they talked about putting it out of print. Why? The distributor only paid the press once a year, and printing expenses were draining them of income. Luckily, my publisher, in a staggering act of generosity, reconsidered.

~~~~

Once Joni started writing from the jet fuel of romantic hurt, could anything be the same? The jet fuel that launched her work was perceived to be depressing when it was often anything but. A good percentage of *Blue* was funny. Not hilarious, but playful, wry. Those lines turned up everywhere—"Loved me so naughty"— but listeners didn't often hear the line like that. The tone of her voice didn't guide us how to feel. Instead, she gave up her control, trusting that the work itself would know more than she did, which is just what happens when language is exact. It leaves room for ambiguity, contradictory feeling. It wasn't hers anymore. It belonged to music, to how people took it into their bloodstream.

One afternoon I started writing about my childhood neighborhood, especially Mrs. Fox, the stylish lady with the Paul McCobb chairs next door, who couldn't look over to our yard without some judgment, whether it was the petroleum blue of our shutters or the grade of the stones around our plants. I was probably trying too hard to write something of substance—I was holding on too hard. And one day I compiled a list of descriptions that came to me when I conjured her up. The descriptions implied a voice, present tense instead of past. And the sound that came back was funny, though that had never been my aim. I'd been writing fiction in order to escape myself, but maybe there was no compulsion to do that anymore. For a second I didn't recognize that person on the page. I felt a little embarrassed by that person and wanted to change everything about him: how he held his arms at his side, the cut of his jacket around his shoulders, his neck inside his shirt. It was a little like watching a film of myself when I had no idea there had been a camera trained on me. At the same time, I could see that in writing about myself, I had already left myself behind. This figure was no longer me but an avatar. Sure, he had some of my markings and traits, but he was never as unique as he thought he was, which is probably true of all of us. There is sadness in that knowing—relief too. How little one life is. How vast and intricate and full of mythical heights and depths.

My name would be on the piece, as well as the eventual book that sprung from it, *Famous Builder*, a collection of essays about self-making through the frame of my childhood infatuations. But only I knew the real story behind it. I could set it free.

~~~~~

If this era had a tuning, it would be the tuning of *Hejira*'s "Black Crow," a voicing that isn't used in any other Joni song. The notes are so wide that it sounds like the strings are going to slacken and fall out of tune at any second. And that is the allure of the song—not its lyrics, which contain no precise descriptions or similes, no references to farmhouses burning down or hexagrams of the heavens. It's barely held together, but the speaker keeps on going forward. People loved you for going forward in impossible conditions, for going out onstage when your throat was sore or putting a sentence to the page when it felt like all eyes were waiting for you to fail, without knowing that accident and glitch are exactly where life begins. The song never slips out of the web it spins. The melody never touches ground, like a crow in flight. The music is its own undoing, and it doesn't solve one thing. Though musically it keeps on lifting, surprising, electric guitar in atonal bursts. And maybe that's the most that we can hope for in a life: little innovations, sparks, a shock of lightning torching up a tree.

THE CIRCLE GAME

~~~~~~~~

WE WALKED UP THE STAIRCASE TO THE PERFORMANCE SPACE, treads too shallow for my shoes. In a town of small spaces, this one was smaller than most: the second floor of a Cape Cod across the street from Cumberland Farms called The Jungle at Tropical Joe's. We came in our T-shirts so we wouldn't lose too much sweat. The ceiling was pitched. The walls, from what I could see in the dark, were bright colors, a New England approximation of a Yucatán beach town, which was more convincing than it sounds. Everywhere I turned there was a figure of an iguana, patterning the bar, the buckled wooden floor. I even caught one on the ceiling. *Firetrap*, I thought, but I was courting disaster to even have that thought. Sometimes I thought about how easy it would be for the whole town to catch fire, embers swarming from one building to the next like honeybees aflame, blown by the wind swept down from the Gulf of Maine. Fire haunted the town every time a siren howled in the middle of the night.

Friends had described John Kelly's *Paved Paradise* as being

"Joni Mitchell in drag," but that sounded reductive, and without any additional direction from them, I knew whatever he did would be more complicated than that. Since the early 1980s, he'd been visible and acclaimed in New York for his performance work and visual art. His sensibility took its energy from all sorts of artists on the fringes, from Caravaggio to Egon Schiele to Antonin Artaud to Jean Cocteau. So for me there was no question his performance would have more layers than my friends' description. All anyone needed to do was look at the poster. He was no copy of Joni. He wasn't interested in facsimile. His expression was more aloof than Joni's, more ethereal, more scattered, less interested in one-to-one conversation. There was plenty of John Kelly in that poster in spite of the straight blond wig parted in the center, right out of the *Clouds* period. Similarities ended there, even though I could imagine Joni approving of the skirt. From what I could tell, the character we were about to see had a more complicated relationship to gender than was in vogue at the time: this wasn't simply a "man" performing as a "woman," which was true of even the edgiest drag performers back then. The performance did not presume a gender orientation. It was ahead of its time by decades. It had its origins in Joni, but it was as much interested in awkwardness, slippage, the gaps between performance and the inner life that queer people negotiated, sometimes with success, sometimes not, a hundred times a day. Part homage, part parody.

When Joni came to his concert at the Fez, another tiny club in a New York City basement, the two of them watched each other from across another tight room, inevitably overheated. It's hard not to wonder who had it harder. John, who knew that Joni was out there in the dark with her entourage, scrutinizing every tuning, phrasing, lyrical accuracy. Or Joni, who heard the audience laughing at patter lifted from the live *Miles of Aisles* recording, this younger version of herself a stranger. Did it feel like she was among her fans? Did a good number think she was of another era, ridiculous? *Was* she ridiculous? And what was it like to sit among people who kept looking back at her to catch the look on her face? Was that the most intense pressure? She likely remembered her mother remarking about this whenever she sat in the audience, whenever people around her got word that she was Joni's mother. How would the air in the room have changed if Joni herself, for one minute, allowed her face to drift off, look less than interested or amused?

So many gay and lesbian people next to her, in front of her. It might have been a gay bar—she'd been in some of those back in the days when she went to bars. Did she wonder why these gay people were drawn to her? What was it about her that drew in a similar, though not quite identical, audience, the same audience that went crazy for all those women with sprayed hair, lacquered emotion, stylized expressions? She was *authentic*—or so she believed. What did they see in her that she couldn't see about herself? When she looked in the mirror, she saw herself, but maybe others were seeing Judy Garland, updated. But she was no victim. *She* dropped her suitors, not the other way around. And she didn't *belt*—or let her eyes mist or wobble her lip onstage.

And then there came a point when she forgot about herself, her reputation, her legacy, the faces and the bodies crowding the room. And it wasn't because she'd written the songs or whom she'd loved when she'd written them. She was listening to songs, pure, floating in space, shared. Listening to talent, the control of his tenor, the way he wobbled his vibrato into siren territory, which began in satire and ended up somewhere else, beyond funny, beyond categorization: interplanetary. She caught herself tearing up. She caught herself tearing up again, and twice more before the encore, and when John walked off the stage, any doubts she'd had when she'd walked in through the door had all gone up in smoke. She crushed out her cigarette. She stood, carried a mountain dulcimer backstage to John, so shy and grateful to take the instrument into his hands. The smile on his face. The smile on hers as someone raised the camera and took photos of the two of them, so alike and different at once, side by side.

~~~~

Honestly, I didn't care if it was Joni singing or someone else. This wasn't a time in which she was performing much, and I just wanted to hear her songs in a room with others. It had been so long. And I wanted to behold risk. To perform her songs in the late 1990s was to court gall, audacity, and cluelessness, and with a few exceptions, the exercise ended up in disappointment and, more often, failure. The prevailing notion was that the songs were Joni's alone. When people performed them, they didn't retune their guitars; they flattened them out harmonically and streamlined their odd moves into songs that sounded like a thousand other songs. As if they'd had high hopes for complexity, couldn't maintain that standard, and had to settle into some in-between place too weird to be conventional: alternative high school children sent to a boarding school where they were forced to endure long days in blazers and penny loafers.

Our seats put us right beside the stage, uncomfortably front and center. I saw guitars, two guitars, lined up on their stands. When John Kelly performed, would he take the time to retune the guitar from one song to the next? Would he save the most demanding songs for the end or intersperse them? I already believed I knew the answer—he was pushing against something. The work wouldn't have gotten such attention unless he were pursuing a little mess, but I'd prepared myself to be let down, at least some. This was Provincetown in July, the height of summer. 1998. Lightning flared over the harbor, and beyond that, the elusive Middle Cape, geography tricking you into thinking it was Boston when Boston was 82.7 miles farther away. There were only thirteen weeks to the season, and no business ever made the money it hoped to. For that reason alone, every purchase of an ice-cream cone or overdyed sweatshirt felt a little more charged than they otherwise would have been.

Would "Black Crow" have the power to pull the tourists off Commercial Street? "Don't Interrupt the Sorrow"?

The space filled. The chair felt impossibly hard on my butt, and I had a hard time keeping my left leg still. I shook and I shook. I looked around to see if there was anybody I knew in those chairs, if anyone loved Joni as much as I did.

~~~~~

I was thinking of John singing as Joni, Joni leaving the constraints of "woman" as the room filled up, as people sat too close, legs pressed together. When the room was too tight, how could you not want to break out, break out into another form? When Joni twisted herself into an invented character's role, she took the song to a different dimension. She was able to draw on qualities she wouldn't have been able to capture if she were singing a character more closely aligned with herself: menace, disinhibition, slyness, entitlement. The relief of trying on another voice, pulling oneself through another's pants and sleeves. In "Coyote," for instance, it's tempting to let the secondary character run away with the song, but the narrator has to take it back, finally. That's part of the joy. He's been let out of his room for a few seconds: *Go back inside and leave me to myself.* When he asks the speaker why she'd gotten so drunk, why she'd led him on, it's easy to confuse that voice with the primary speaker's. But she's in charge now. She's the hitcher who doesn't get attached, doesn't show emotion, a more grown-up version of the speaker in "Cactus Tree."

The characters kept coming into my imagination as people poured in. Not just cameo appearances but full songs. "A Chair in the Sky," in which she's singing of Charles Mingus's last days, thinking about what he'll miss, what he'd like to be in his next life. Though the musing is built of lists, almost mundane in its everydayness, the act of it is profound given his belief in reincarnation.

Similarly, "God Must Be a Boogie Man." The opening pages of Mingus's autobiography, *Beneath the Underdog,* but in Joni's voice, laying out the three parts of the psyche. The sweet side; the ferocious, reactive side; and the one in the middle, trying to make peace between the two parts at war.

"Two Grey Rooms," in which the speaker is a gay man, reportedly based on a friend of Werner Fassbinder, the German director. It's hard not to hear that voice as a version of Joni's own predicament, written, as it was, at a low point in her visibility. "No one knows I'm here." Would she have been able to say those words if she hadn't taken a leap across categories? Down there, beneath the window, the man the character's been in love with for thirty years. Shirt unbuttoned on a hot day, sexy.

And finally, "Free Man in Paris." Another gay man, but this time stepping into the suit of an unnamed David Geffen, one of her two managers. The character doesn't simply dream of leaving the record business behind but lusts to meet "a very good friend." Outing him then before the culture had even coined that word. A warm song on the surface, breezy as a drink on a summer afternoon, but upon closer inspection, there's thunder coming. See the clouds on the horizon? Aggression—aggression in its conception? Outing your manager in 1974, angry at the steady pressure to produce a hit, to sell more records, to stay vital in the game. *I'll show you what a hit looks like*, and she makes a hit out of him. Number twenty-two on the Billboard Hot 100. *There. Now what? I wrote a song about you. Do you want another?*

~~~~~

John as Joni came out on the stage to hardy applause. The shy Joni face: he looked down, looked up, and started fingerpicking—quietly. He was tall, top of the head too close to the ceiling. There was nothing easy about it, nothing rote—all of it poised on the edge of falling apart, nothing pretty. He was but five feet away from me—closer? I saw his hands, his long, lean hands, turning the tuning pegs, his mouth moving, even the spit flying through the air when he sang. There was laughter in the room, but it wasn't exactly comfortable laughter, because not everyone was laughing at the same thing. Some people laughed especially emphatically because they knew the reference from the album, always arcane, and wanted to show others they got the reference—how could there not be some competition in a room full of Joni fans? But to laugh too hard seemed wrong, all wrong, a major key/standard tuning wish for togetherness of the cheapest sort, an all-on-the-same-page attitude that wanted to smooth out discomfort. A sweep of the melody on "Blue" and the voice was unguarded longing, maybe even more unguarded than Joni herself: less constructed, more willing to be off, to be bad, even testing out the word *bad*, the laziness at the heart of it. A love letter to Joni, but that was only the beginning. It spun off into a more daring and confusing and entirely involving performance. I felt it coming up through my legs, through my back and shoulders, and into my face. I might have had on a face that was smiling widely or confused. Did others? I tried to look around, but the houselights were too hot and bright on my face—I couldn't see anything. We were up so close that we might have been part of the show, and to look around too much would have pulled me out of the moment, pulled others out too. For the sweetest stretch, we were very far away from what was most oppressive about Provincetown: the lights, the noise, the long lines at Spiritus Pizza for slices or ice cream, the traded looks, the jangling *want*. We were far away from death, which was still the central story of that place even in the late 1990s, a few years after antivirals thinned out the obituary page of the newspaper. Soon there would be no reason to read the original town newspaper, and it would fold.

I've already said it, but if I had been given a list of Joni songs I'd wanted to hear performed, I wouldn't have chosen "The Circle

Game." As close to a conventional song as she'd ever write, designed
for others to cover it, in line with "Urge for Going" with its reassur-
ing melody and chords. John as Joni might have sensed my opinion,
even though at an early point in my life, I'd adored that song the
way I'd adored "Puff, the Magic Dragon," its misfit combination
of hope, sweetness, and a broken heart. Not the broken heart of
adulthood, which was about loss, but something more mysterious:
not knowing what, if anything, would become of a life and mourning the loss to come. Who was singing "The Circle Game" when
I first heard it—where? And who were those voices on the chorus,
the mess of them, almost in unison but not quite? Was it a church
song? It sounded like a church song, at least the kind we sang, and
maybe that was why John as Joni turned to me and sang only to
me. For the next five minutes, everyone was gone from the room,
even my partner, and I didn't miss him, which was curious in
our relationship of anticipatory missing. John as Joni looked in
my eyes, I looked back, and I didn't feel the urge to look away, the
fear of domination or submission. I was protected, or maybe I was
protecting John as Joni by listening, by being present. We made a
circle around us, and it was turning like a wheel the size of the room
and beyond. And it felt too many things at once to name while we
were in it. Joni singing to me. Joni fan to Joni fan. Queer person to
queer person. One musician singing to a former musician, trying
to bring him back home. Four layers at once, five, and in any other
circumstance, it would've been too much, but the stage made it safe,
the stage gave us the constraints that allowed intimacy to happen,
the kind of intimacy that would have been harder to achieve if
we'd been sitting in chairs, talking to each other at a table, across
a candle.

What do you call such a thing if it isn't a blessing?

No.

A blessing feels off, sentimental, part of a context that never did right by queer people. Grace? A moment of? Even that felt off.

There isn't a word. Who needs a word for an experience that stretched out the definition of the old words until they became something else?

What felt unique: his gesture didn't require anything of me. It came without ask or a want. And it came unbidden, unexpected. This didn't always happen.

The room held still for a time. The colors of Mexico. The high peak of the ceiling. Lanterns hanging down, low enough to bop your skull.

Then John as Joni lifted his head, the lights changed, the song over, and the rest of the show went on, impeccably. I felt my face becoming one with the other faces, which was all right by me. My skin cooled a little. I was no longer chosen. One could bear the hot lights of that position for only so long.

~~~~

Two summers passed, and I was sitting before the actual Joni at the FleetBoston Pavilion, an outdoor amphitheater fronting on Boston's inner harbor. She was in apricot and pink, in a hooded jacket both rugged and petalled, as if she'd pushed out of herself from a bulb in the ground and was still getting used to the lights. Part plant, part fish, part bird. Behind her, across the harbor, the planes of Logan Airport lined up for takeoff. Colorless sky. Cold sea, eelgrass, treated sewage, laundry detergent, iodine—the water's aroma strong, though not at all unpleasant. Two rows in from the stage. A breeze blew over my face and the faces behind me. Snugged into our coats. Another outdoor amphitheater—it seemed impossible to see her any other way, as if her performance could no longer be contained by mere walls. Through sheer determination, a few months back, I'd scored second-row seats. I'd been taut as a piano wire since, convinced that calamity was going to happen between then and now. I was still taut from my neck down to my spine.

From her position in front of the orchestra, she said she was going to "put the guitar down, step away from the piano, and just enjoy singing"—but that was to be expected. There was a script behind the evening—a live performance of the *Both Sides Now* album, a preview of the nascent *Travelogue*—but that didn't mean some didn't wish the seventy-piece orchestra away and a piano to roll out on its own, Joni sitting down at the bench to sing "My Old Man."

Such as the person beside me. That person, a stranger, seemed to think that by yelling at frequent intervals, she could urge a different kind of concert out of Joni: less orchestral, more individual, skeletal. Every song, including the patter before it, was met with animal sounds. The animal sounds weren't about rousing the crowd to attention. The crowd was already tuned to the music, even though they might have missed the Jonis they knew best, whether they were *Ladies of the Canyon* or *Turbulent Indigo*. This night asked something different of Joni, of the person next to me. And if Joni was going to stick to a script, the onus was on her to refresh the album's phrasing, which had already needled into our cortices.

146

And forty-five minutes into the concert, Joni walked stage left for intermission.

"JONI," the stranger screamed, bloodcurdling now, as if love meant ruining yourself, giving your throat lining nodules. And performing that damage for others to see just so they knew what you were willing to do to yourself.

Joni once said that the audience is a dragon, and the first five rows are the eyes of the beast, and they telegraph emotions all the way back to the tail, which doesn't even know it's subject to their control. But rather than hurrying away from the dragon, she stopped and turned to us. And looked not at the heckler—whom I'd begun to think of as such—but right at me. My face must have looked confused, pleading. Happily shocked. A simultaneity of emotion that couldn't be boxed into any single expression. Did she recognize that expression?

Four seconds. Five? Ten? We rested inside each other's gaze, neither looking away.

I know you.

And the Joni who saw my face was still riding the music. Later she'd describe the concert as "the perfect wave, shooting the pipe from one end to the other." But now she didn't look at the heckler's face but at mine—she wanted to make things better for me. Then we were bemused together, smiling. We were talking with our faces, thinking the same thought: *Why do people want like this? Such hunger.* But she seemed to be looking at herself too, as if she were a person who had made such mistakes. She'd made a fool of herself for love too.

Had I?

In *Aspects of the Novel*, E. M. Forster writes about the difference between clock time and emotional time, or, as he calls it, the life in time and the life in values: "Something which is measured not by minutes or hours but by intensity, so that when we look at our past it does not stretch back evenly but piles up into a few notable pinnacles, and when we look at the future it seems sometimes a wall, sometimes a cloud, and sometimes a sun, but never a chronological chart." And if that is the case, that was this moment that recalled it. It opened up for hours and swept backward and forward until I was clean.

Did I need blessing then, protection? I believed in the life I'd made, as if it were something *out there*, something I'd watched and evaluated as I would a performance. It is easy to convince yourself you're living the life you want instead of the one you've settled for. Who walks around carrying the latter on their back? It's unbearable. It's heavier than water. You want to stand up straight. And even though I'd have questions about the second half of the concert—the orchestra's occasional out-of-tuneness, too much bombast and grandeur on "Ludwig's Tune," which required quiet and simplicity in order to land—I felt the two sides of myself drawing closer across a rift. What had I forgotten? Up on the stage, the lights doused Joni's face in orange and pink. She'd become the bird that had already flown.

THE JUNGLE LINE

~~~~~~~~

SHADBUSH, SASSAFRAS, JUNEBERRY, BLACK CHERRY, HOLLY: MARI-time forest. Layers of heavy minerals, the color of garnet, swirled into the white sand beach. Monarch butterflies over the dunes, high and low, not in groups but on their own, feeding on flower nectar. Early autumn, workers racing the boardwalks to fix some problem: a crack in the pool lining, rotten shower stall, soft plank in the decking. The sun so potent, it might have been a charac-ter, penetrating the skin. Leaves too. I'd never been in leaves like that. Thick leaves always curated your looking. They softened hard edges; they hid what didn't want to be seen, which was a lot. They were falling too, a few of them. Nearly all of them patched with red and gold, some desiccation around the edges. It was September, the late days of the month. Still warm, but swirled with cool air. Summer coming to a close.

The houses, usually full in summer, were empty now, and that was why I'd brought my teaching prep out here to Fire

Island. When the houses around our house were empty, I felt my aloneness less, forgot that I missed human touch. There was no reason to miss human touch if it wasn't part of the range of options. Out here during the week, once the contractors took the ferry back to Sayville on the mainland, the human world receded. Late afternoon. Offseason. And my senses turned to animals, woods, water—all the things I missed when I was back in the city.

I went to the store, but the shelves were full of open spaces. The owners already preparing for shutting down in a month, only stocking the basics. If one wasn't up to the challenge of making do with less, then there wasn't much point in being here. I liked having to deal with fewer options when I was used to having options. Fewer options. Isn't that why I was out here rather than in our apartment in Manhattan, where in order to deal with the overstimulation of city life, I'd carved out a smaller hoofprint over time, a square of blocks from West Fourteenth to Twenty-Fifth? By 2007 I'd turned the city into a small town, small as our one-bedroom apartment. Weren't small apartments possible because, in theory, people only went to bed in them, spending the rest of the day in coffee shops, bars, the office, meeting rooms in church basements?

But car horns, the constant low rumble, sidewalk life—the neurotic fixation on the twenty minutes in front of them. It was so easy to be another placeholder in that hive. So easy to think you were unique when you passed the men at the bar, who cracked up, threw back their heads, and clapped once, as if to signal they'd always been in on the joke, and you'd always be outside.

~~~~

The skin between the inside and outside was so thin, the trees might have been in the living room and vice versa. The sound of the ocean, five hundred feet on the other side of the dune, filling the kitchen with a roar, but friendly. Friendly lion.

Here I was as deep in my life as I'd ever been. I wasn't thinking about it from above, from the height of our apartment. I wasn't already thinking about March when I was in September. But how far I was from my Provincetown life, which in its best years was a life of new people all the time, of not knowing what was next. I loved Fire Island for the way the human intertwined with the world of animals and plants. No cars or roads—instead, raised boardwalks with white stripes painted along the edge. Streetlights? Nonexistent. Deer wandering around with astonishing nonchalance. Rabbits, box turtles, snakes, Fowler's toads in the places you couldn't see. Maybe it was simply concealment that I was drawn to, a place that refused to prune and tame itself for convention, the sake of sunlight and display. When you walked at night, you had to tune yourself to your muscles, nerves, and senses. Especially true in the Meat Rack (also known as the Judy Garland Memorial Forest), if you were walking from Cherry Grove back to the Pines, in which aiming a flashlight down the path was not just gauche but lacking in substance, character. You had to look, squint, listen for the sounds around you. That rustling at night? Monster? No, just some guy deep in the bayberry with a cigarette aglow, looking to hook up with a bearded daddy.

During the day, sunlight poured onto the beach, south-facing, Caribbean. It went through your pupils all the way to the back of your head until your vision went deep red, veins branching. The ocean was similarly intense. Bodysurf a wave and you risked getting driven into the slope, sinuses filling, your neck jolted into shock, electric. It was said that the son of one long-term resident broke his back by doing just that and was a quadriplegic for the rest of his life.

If a place could be as strange as one of Joni's songs, then this was it. The beach was as beautiful as any beach I'd ever seen, holly forest up against the secondary dune. The sun struck it as if it had waited all night to do so and couldn't wait to saturate and heat it up, to get down into the cool, dark spaces between trees. But something was *off* about the place, something wonky. It tried to be glamorous with its mid-century modern houses, some with flat roofs, others with soaring peaks, but the land would never be as trim and tidy as any part of the Hamptons or even Loveladies on Long Beach Island, its nearest relative. There was too much greenery, burgeoning, creeping. The few lawns looked wrong. It suggested a swamp, an Everglades, but wrenched out of its expected geography, lifted to northern latitudes: litter in the woods, propane tanks exposed, the occasional sagging electric line, summer downpours turning the single dirt road into a stagnant, muddy lake that wouldn't evaporate for weeks. But this low-level chaos was central to its appeal. Beauty required rot—it was its closest sibling. Rot kept its participants awake. And in that way the landscape felt like the correlative to so many Joni songs. The meticulousness of those songs! Every second wanted to be extraordinary, but the extraordinary also required some mess for the sake of contrast: slack strings, dissonance, more words shoveled into the line than a melody to contain them. They weren't designed to make you feel comfortable. You couldn't simply listen to them on autopilot as you could so many other songs. But they, like this place, made you love them for their sense of reaching, for embodying imperfection and thus horror. The sublime is never easy, because the longer you look and listen to it, the more it is pointing to decay, endings, and death.

Not to mention that none of it was guaranteed beyond next week. In just the last year, the water had eroded the bank along the bay, exposing the gnarled roots of the trees, a major footpath gone, ledge worn away by the tides. Every winter, storms of longer duration stole away some beachside pools, staircases, decks, leaving mangled wreckage in their wake. It was impossible to calculate how much time the place had left, even when a dredge churned fresh sand out onto the beach every few years, a masquerade of safety.

~~~~~

The neighbors' pool speakers popped on at eleven a.m., as they did every day of the week. The predictability didn't make things easier. If anything, the clock made it worse: we walked around the house, absurdly tense, waiting for the moment when the bass line vibrated the windows in their frames. It involved a ritual, a walk to their front door, anxious, never pleasant. Would you mind turning the speakers down? Thanks. And a reluctant, disgruntled yes, after which an interval of twenty minutes passed before the music went even louder.

It probably didn't help matters that I was never the one who made that trip. Why? I was afraid; I didn't have the spine, which made me feel like shit about myself. And maybe on an unspoken level, I thought that sound was a complicated issue: how we manage it, who has the right to it. How many gay people, especially those with effeminate voices, have been told to shut up? Loud voices, loud music—people were scared, people were strong, people were saying, through other means, *You won't crush me.*

"I hate it here," said my partner one day, his voice grinding in his throat. Then we were in the flood, as if a dam had been breached. He wanted me to agree, and I couldn't. It was my fault that we were here, though he never said as much. It was understood between the two of us that I loved the house more than he did, loved its mid-century architecture, the plants and birds. Part of what made it a challenge was that the island was a place where everyone knew everyone—its population felt stable, closed. Doors didn't swing open so widely here, even if you had a certain degree of visibility in other worlds. It was a place where you spent only weekends, dropped by occasionally. A pressure valve for high-powered city lives, and we were expecting it to be habitual, routine, the equivalent of attending an ongoing underwear party in a seersucker shirt even if you weren't averse to lots of sex. Socially, it was the opposite of Provincetown, where fans of my partner's work would walk right into the yard, sometimes up to the back door of the kitchen, unannounced, asking if they could hug him, which he invariably let them do. In such circumstances, how could he not hug back? But it was one of the reasons why Provincetown, which had once felt more like home than where we'd grown up, was no longer a refuge. Too many eyes. Gratitude and intrusion walk a very fine line sometimes.

And now here we'd taken ourselves to a place that operated under a different set of conditions. A culture of parties sounds like fun, but it has a dark side. It's not concerned with anybody on the perimeter. On some level it has to work like that, or you can't invite those twenty people over for a spontaneous party after the bars close. Your happiness happens against someone else's. Under the circumstances, how could the person on the other side of that not hear the pool music as aggression, the parties as against you personally? You lose a little of your generosity, your perspective. You own a house. You forget how lucky you are to be in the extraordinary place, to have such problems.

A gruesome smell wafted over the backyard. Rugged, grainy, physical. If the smell had had a color, it would have been yellow, but so yellow that it was impossible to tell it from a lurid brown. Stronger on some days but always immediate, nearby. Eye-watering. It had its origins in the natural but smelled, what, chemical? Ammonia? A human body? It wouldn't have been so outlandish to imagine human body parts stashed underneath a pool deck, especially when another neighbor routinely screamed bloody murder for extended periods after midnight. I googled primal scream therapy and believed the explanation I read made sense, but it sounded too neat for what I heard, which was someone turning himself inside out, gutting himself, as if he'd had enough of being human and was ready to be an animal.

One morning we were raking the leaves in the backyard, and the tines hit something hard, as hard as poured concrete. We tapped it with our handles again, first one and then the other. We pulled back some leaves. Dug deeper and pulled back some more. Maggots over grayed fur, quivering, multitudinous. It took longer than usual to process. We leapt away, running inside the house for towels to cover our eyes and noses. We went back out again. A dead deer with a severed leg, and how many months had it festered out there just on the other side of the outdoor shower? A creature who would have lived if not for humans, if there hadn't been so many raised boardwalks to run into, to leap over and miss.

What else had we allowed our senses to miss? We were so far from our bodies, it was as if we'd been walking around with broken feet and hadn't looked down to see the bruise.

~~~~

Maybe what I'm not getting down here is that we were trying to build a home together. We'd had a home before, but everything about the Provincetown house was haunted, not just by the life my partner and *his* former partner had built—all the signs, ceramic pitchers, and hutches collected at Vermont flea markets—but by all the people who'd cooked and slept there back to 1790. This was a house that hadn't had much past in it. We'd had enough past. We were soaked in it. To be a gay man in 2007 was to have nothing but the past and its weight, but this place felt light, new. Here everything was determinedly new, if a charcoal-colored mid-century modern ranch built in the late 1960s could be called new. It was too casual to be taken seriously, when the literary life surrounding us said, *You are serious. You must maintain that.* We could buy things for the house together, a painting for the wall, a rice paper light fixture, four black Eames chairs around the glass dining table. The meaning of us as a couple could be found in those things, all the occasions we marked by deciding on *that* together. Two points of view, fused. That felt precious to me twelve years into our relationship. It was startling to me that it took that long.

~~~~

A pool was in view: high-end lounge chairs on the deck, tropical plants sprouting out of pocked ceramic pots. Inside, couples sat across the table from each other, passing teak bowls around, lifting glasses, pouring more wine. Standard Hotels–style runway music played softly on the sound system. It was one of those situations in which I had to remind myself that I loved being with people, loved hearing their stories, loved making them laugh. And yet my back was stiff, the roof of my mouth so dry, my intestines unsettled. Around the table were people I had no connection with, though I'd tried to form them. Certainly we all knew what it was like to feel ostracized. Maybe I'd gotten to be good when it came to spotting a certain kind of person: the one with harm in his eyes and the ready laugh he used to cover it. The one who walked into the room and thought, *Now how am I going to control these people; how am I going to hold on to my power?* Eyes darting for a vulnerable face like a hunter first stepping onto a woodland path.

It was harder to have fun when we'd lost the thing that had held us together. We'd lost a vocabulary of understanding. What were we if not that: a sense of the world that was never on our side. Our community had stopped dying en masse from AIDS; drugs kept people alive longer than they expected to be alive, though we didn't yet know how long that was. We no longer had to live in heightened alert. Who could have seen this ten years before? All we had was our ability to take care of one another, and nobody knew how to talk about a new reality, which had shifted as quickly as a storm scudding across the bay. I thought of polio being eradicated by a vaccine in a sugar cube, the quickness of its delivery after so much suffering. Shouldn't we have been able to talk about the people we missed? How it felt to survive when the only thing we were certain of was that we had no future—it couldn't be counted upon, and if there was anything like a future, it was one in which we were diminished, compromised. It was too much to stay in that place. Some preferred to behave as if the worst of those years had never happened, as if it were beyond our capacity to comprehend it emotionally and physically—it was still corroding our psychic metal. Our ability to process and understand narrowed as the years went on, the calendar slipping off the wall. Humans forget, not just out of laziness but as a survival tool. It's *work*. And a new formality arrived as a way to keep conversation from getting to be too specific and intimate. The challenge was to make sure that at any dinner party, no conversation mattered too much, even though it was taxing to be in that place for very long; it took discipline. It would have been easier to summarize string theory.

The evening required a different set of social skills than I'd been prepared for. It involved a practiced cynicism, a dry wit learned from old Hollywood movies or *The Sopranos*, a deadened affect. If you didn't play along, if you said something too earnest or sweet, it would ruin everything. It would mean you were trying to take control, and who were you to think that you could determine the agenda when you were only an invited guest, when you'd picked up persimmon bread from the store rather than make it yourself? You were inviting the possibility of change. You were throwing out the script for all when it had originated long before your arrival on the front step, at the door, and your job was to find it, *learn* it so that there would never be awkwardness ever again.

Because if *you* were awkward, you made everyone else awkward. It spread like a head cold that turned into the flu.

Awkwardness, the human poison.

Awkwardness, the language of gay childhood, which is spent trying to glue up the gaps between uncertainty and the seemingly coherent culture around one.

That night was all awkwardness. Fork hitting glass, candle flames sifting shapes on the ceiling above us. A storm coming in from the west, lightning, though still the script remained supreme. We were not to make mention of the storm, of falling barometric pressure. The short hairs standing up on the backs of our necks.

Maybe it would have been more bearable if we'd been able to acknowledge the electric undercurrent of the night, which didn't want to be collective deadness but the erotic, which can't be contained, which falls outside of clear narrative tracks. A hand on someone's back, a walk into someone's bedroom, door closing behind you, or maybe not. Your partner pairing off with someone else in the next bedroom. But the prospect typically remained a prospect. Faces and hands tensed up—who would walk outside and start kissing someone by the edge of the pool? When? Who would get left out? Certainly someone needed to be left out; wasn't that necessary? Everyone on the lookout so they wouldn't miss the signal, so they wouldn't be on the outskirts, even as they weren't sure they wanted to be there anymore.

I walked over to the window. Six miles across the bay were the mainland and its lights and trees. The federal courthouse in Central Islip, the only tall building in Suffolk County. Wide bay all but a foot or two deep outside the ferry channel. Once our lives were too unsettled for dinner parties. Slapdash, too rushed, chaotic—who knew when somebody was going to fall ill, need to say good night early? Some of us had the bodies of older people, though we were in our twenties and thirties. This didn't mean that people didn't have fun, but fun had a purpose to it, a mission. Fun had teeth. Fun chewed away the corpse of death and gave us a reprieve.

Now, though, people too easily fell into old family structures—or patterns from high school. They gave back the ugliness that was once given to them. You could see it in their body language.

I caught my right shoulder curving inward. I thought, *This is what a creature does when he doesn't feel safe in his space, in his body.* I pushed it backward, but it wouldn't stay back against the chair. For the rest of the evening, I repeated the procedure. I pushed it back.

~~~~~

The all-night party transformed the beach into a movie set. The birds, moths, and mosquitoes didn't know what to do with the music, the hot lights, the dancers thrashing and frenetic beneath them. Usually they got close, veered off, went back in again, dazed. Two a.m. Drugs transformed the air—it didn't even matter if you were taking them or not. Every living creature appeared to absorb them: Willows took them up through the water in their root systems and swelled, splayed open. The leaves got thicker, more liquid. Birds' voices fell down an octave and pooled. As for the borderlines in Joni's song of that same name? Gone. Nothing was pinned down.

~~~~~

The deer tipped over a trash can, tonguing the containers for rotten food smells, coffee grounds, and Milky Way wrappers. When had they lost their fear of us? When the plates of cut-up celery stalks and carrots were left out by front gates? When people started to talk to them, not in the voices of threat but with awe? When human beings became more than creatures attached to rifles and bows? That was it. A collective nervous system shifted. Their bodies relaxed in a whole new way, and when they felt it, they could look back at people. At some point we were theirs. It was *their* habitat. And when it was clear that we weren't going to fell them with arrows, we mattered less. They set the perspective, despite the carts rushing down the boardwalks, the hollers and hoots that lashed the night.

As for the people: some were delighted. To see deer this close—deer that didn't dart off—was to see that they had singular personalities: that one bold, that one playful and shy. Antlers that looked almost as nice as the white papier-mâché ones we'd pinned to the wall. They were like dogs. Yellow Labs, but with more mystery and gravitas, as if they'd mated with space aliens. They all had faces. They had individual character. When I watched them, they pulled me into the present, with the business of their living, their own rules, always opaque to me. Browsing for food at dusk and dawn, taking to the beach and swimming, sometimes at the height of day. Where did they go when it started to rain? Under someone's deck? In some pocket of trees where they closed their eyes and put up with drops on their faces? The possibilities of that question could occupy me for a half hour.

It was late one afternoon, just before the last ferry of the day. I was out here by myself, and as usual, I was rushing around in that hour, sweeping sand into a dustpan, tying twine around newspapers, rushing to the bathroom to put the contact lens solution in my bag. And, oh, *that*—the last minutes of locking up were always hectic in a way they wouldn't be hectic if the island could have been reached by train or car. And just as I locked the front door, I spotted the deer through the mesh fence. Strolling through the empty lot next door like a relaxed moose, brawny and curious but peaceful. Chin up, hide maybe a few shades darker than a younger deer, which suggested age, majesty. But the startling thing? The rack on top of his head: six points. A chandelier? Back to home decor. If he were a man, he'd be a linebacker for the Giants, all muscle and tight hide.

The two of us had the place to ourselves. Everything would have been different if someone had been around to see. To be observed: it would have changed us. The human intrusion. We'd have been watching ourselves: fear of cuteness, fear of stupidity, the anthropomorphic, projection.

He turned to me, walked over to the fence without hesitation. I put my bag down on the deck and met him.

We were standing face-to-face. Only the mesh fence between us, all of two feet apart. Maybe he was expecting me to pass him a celery stalk, but the closest he came to begging was head dipping down. One would think that an animal of that size would have charged if he'd felt like it, just to show me he could do it—humans do some version of that to one another all the time. Why not use that size against me, against human creatures? For the one who lay dying in the backyard, who couldn't have been the only one.

On the day we drove through Montauk last month, I saw a sign by the road: 461 deer collisions since January 1. And who knew where those shocked bodies ended up.

If he had a smell, it was hard to pin down. Wet leaves? Lake? Wood chips? Dark, mossy green—though I don't mean shit. Perhaps my smell was extreme to him, not how I smelled to other humans.

I talked, but only some questions. At some point, he understood that I wasn't going to feed him, and once that idea rolled away, we were somewhere different: a pocket of deep interest. A circle of attention, mutual. The space between us something to protect. One step closer and we couldn't possibly see each other.

His eyes as brown as a chocolate bar. Different beings, but standing on the same spot of earth at the same time. Seven miles out from the mainland. 73.1 latitude, 52.5 miles east of New York City.

We were standing still, watching each other like scientists. Scratching in the treetops above us. A cardinal? Gray catbird on the ground, restless but productive.

I didn't want to step out of this moment; he didn't seem to either. Four o'clock getting closer—people dragging bags, wheels clattering the spaces between the planks of the boardwalk. But I had to leave. There was a doctor's appointment in the city tomorrow, and I was flying to see Bobby in Miami.

I told him goodbye just the way I would say it to a person.

And then I was weeping on my walk and didn't know how I'd fallen into this space. My sleeve was rough as I dragged it across my face. Maybe it was just that he was still standing there, as if inviting me to stay, to come back into the circle we'd made, and I was failing him. I was failing the largest moment in my life, because I needed language to understand, and the right words didn't exist for this. *Shining animal*: too poetic. Irony didn't work either—cynical, reflexive, cowardly, though it pretended to have intellect, rigor. When all else failed, I was practical. I buttoned up my shirt and shut down—it was the safest place to be until I could understand myself again.

I was hurrying away from love, and I had done that before.

~~~~

A week passed.

I might have been processing the song on some level before I heard it, but when I picked out its melody and chords, I started walking toward it. I picked up speed. I didn't want to lose it now that the sound was so near.

Or I didn't want it to be illusion.

It came from a house I never would have paid attention to at any other time, a flavorless rental in vertical light gray wood, some of it softened and swiped with green mildew. Lounge chair turned on its side. Scraped lot, no vegetation growing through the sand. But there was Joni at the sliding glass window. Or Joni's voice: "Strong and Wrong" from *Shine,* the least expected of her albums, as far from the two hit singles of *Court and Spark* as you could get. Not played loud, as in aggression. Not dominating the yards around it but complementing the leaves and green waves. A part of it. The British Columbia version of this spot on Earth. Another Sunshine Coast.

I've always been here, the voice said, but through a different net of words. *What about you?*

I made this, I thought. *This song you're reading.*

My face turned up to the sun. And the sky was so big beyond the pines, it could have split me in two.

~~~~~

I listened to "The Jungle Line" later that night. It sounded darker than I remembered from my teenage years: elemental, urgent, mysterious, part of a life force—but that didn't mean it was uplifting. It made me think of hunting, the urgency of stalking the woods. I pored over the lyrics, tried to decipher the song as if it were possible to make sense of it, feel power and control over it. I reminded myself that relying too much on sense could be a bit of a prison, and maybe the best of Joni's songs resist sense, which believes that life is simpler than it is. The song seems to tell a story, but it actually is a song as a painting, which might be why the painter Rousseau lives at the center of it. Rousseau painting a wall. There is heroin. Mouthpiece spit. A painting—or a dream. A weather system. I thought of it as a weather system.

The facet that captured me the most? The drums: Burundi. "Tambours royaux 'Ingoma.'" The drums sounded completely new and fresh to me, but they also sounded like the song had existed since the beginning of time, and only some had been able to hear it. The drums sounded as personal as a voice—why didn't more pop songs sound like this? The acoustic guitar, the synthesizer—subordinate. The drums touched your jugular, synced up with your heartbeat, its music. They sounded like the inside of your body after you'd taken a long run on the beach and pressed your hands against your ears. Or after you'd come following an extended bout of lovemaking. Both a comfort and a warning.

What did those drums have to do with Joni's other songs? Maybe she found no other way to capture the cluelessness and forgetfulness of white people—the detachment from their bodies, the indifference to history, the refusal to make any connection between the horror of enslavement and how we live now. Or maybe she was also saying something about women, all the ways they find their power and try to get by in a capitalism that imprisons them, uses them up, and discards them, pays them less, forcing them into a series of roles—caricatures drawn from movies—in order to survive.

And there I was, trying to figure it out again and likely missing the point.

I listened to the song every day, maybe four times a day, in part to see who I'd become on the other side of it. It was my prayer of the moment, my psalm. Every time I listened, I felt my cells rearranging, circulating through my arteries and veins, warming me from the inside. It refused stillness. And so I did too.

~~~~~~

L
E
T
T
I
N
G

G
O

~~~~~~

THE WOLF THAT LIVES IN LINDSEY

~~~~~~~~~~~~~~~~~~~~~~~~~~~~

OUT OF NOWHERE HE SAID, "I WROTE A POEM," AND ASKED ME IF I wanted to hear it. I put the student manuscript aside. I needed a break anyway, settled myself on the sofa in a listening posture, my legs folded beneath me. My eagerness had little to do with loyalty or duty or even the love I had for him. I wanted to hear what he'd written, which usually came like a flare on the most unremarkable day, unbidden. This one featured an endangered bird on a stamp, the stamp being its field of enclosure, and took off from there. It sharpened my ear to listen so intently. On most days it was enough to say the poem was gorgeous and to point to a few lines in the third stanza, but I felt I could be of value when I said, "What if you tried to put this one in tercets; what if you changed the order of the last two stanzas?" When he took my suggestions, I felt a kind of satisfaction that I hadn't known before or haven't since. It had little to do with my ego. And to be that close to the making, to be in the room with it, always felt like luck. In such moments I felt a part of poetry, a force of a longer duration than the two of us. The lives we were building weren't static. A new poem could change the walls around us, the floor, the light fixture bolted to the ceiling. Everything within reach— the wine bottle on the end table, the loaf of sourdough with the hard crust—could be enlivened. Life wasn't simply happening to us. We weren't passive. Imagine the room as a glass, a knife hitting the glass, and the whole thing vibrating at once.

And one day I was frustrated, discouraged about the reception of my work. This feeling had been building for months. My novel in progress was long, not in page count but in its ambition. I'd called it *Lumina Harbor*, after the name of the street we'd stayed near in Wilmington, North Carolina, for a spring semester. It was coming on five years since my previous book had been published, and I sensed it was high time to make bigger claims for my work in order to get the kind of review attention where award committees and big bookstores take notice. In simpler terms, I wanted people to read me. It was so easy to disappear. I didn't want my work to disappear, especially because I wanted to reach for a broader audience that didn't compromise my ideals for a kind of work that sounded like me, only me, in terms of description, sonics. *Ideas.* Ideas about belonging and selfhood and the tension between the two. Boundaries, attachment, walking closer, walking away. The body and its secrecies. When I listened to *Court and Spark*, I realized you could still be yourself—you could keep all your chords and musical figures intact but with more vitamins: enhanced, emboldened, *ripped*. My first two books had been well received, but my reputation had settled into a place that suggested that the arc of my career had already been written. This was where I was going to stay for the foreseeable future: on the outer bands of the radar. Once someone had described me as a cult writer, and while I was pleased on some level to hear that term applied to me—it implied that there were enough people out there to care about my books—I also wondered whether it was a way to not take my accomplishments seriously.

But I didn't seem to be able to write the kind of literary novel that stayed within the prescribed margins of what was deemed appealing. It was written in four voices, the briefest of which was a dog speaking from the afterlife. I thought of it as a book of grief: the story of a lost mother and a family's fight to preserve a community against a developer's plans to build an outsized project in the middle of it, crushing wetlands, trees, upending a bird habitat. But according to my writer friends, I'd written a manuscript that was hard to describe, which meant it would be hard to sell, but even the most enthusiastic rejections don't communicate that. They tell you that you are lacking in ways that mean to break your heart. They rightly don't want you to put them in this impossible position again, which is embarrassing, frankly. Who wants to turn anyone down, especially when they've given over their blood to a yearslong project? A rejection often has little to do with the value of art, but it must communicate through the values of art because the language of sales has too much to do with the mysteries of luck to make any sense.

After I'd grown weary of those rejections, I took the book back from my then agent and sent it out in an abbreviated form—one voice instead of four. One hundred twenty pages instead of three hundred. A small press took it on within weeks. I published it under a different title, *The Burning House*, which might have been a figure to think of what had been happening at home, though the book knew much more about any of that before I did.

One Sunday afternoon, on the way home from Fire Island, we exited the Queens-Midtown Tunnel and drove the usual route to Seventh Avenue down East Thirty-Seventh. On the sidewalk underneath a red neon diner sign stood the most magnificent poodle I'd ever seen—more lion than poodle actually. But think of a lion freshly groomed, clipped and clean, with no sign of the costs it took to stand still and endure a blow-dryer pointed at its butt and face for a full hour.

"The poodles of my childhood were nothing like the poodles of today," I said, mysteriously forlorn. I didn't know where that was coming from, other than the picture I had of Suzy Friedman's poodle, who pooped on our lawn right in front of me, Suzy either too defiant or distracted to pick it up. It left a burn mark, the orange of rusted metal, and never quite greened over afterward, no matter how long we watered it.

"That's your opening sentence," my partner said. His voice was as matter-of-fact as a physician who had both diagnosed the illness and prescribed the effective medication in the same sentence.

Then he told me to make a short prose piece about that—no longer than two, three pages. Could even be a paragraph.

The electricity wasn't instantaneous. If anything, it took some time as we headed down Seventh Avenue, in and out through taxis. I felt my heart rate slowing down, my digestive tract going absolutely still. I gazed out at the Hotel Chelsea's white-and-pink neon. The lightning bolt would still hit some seconds away, after we gave over the keys to the garage attendant.

Imagine if a singer-songwriter had been forcing herself to

write pop ballads for years, then someone told her she could write an eight-and-a-half-minute song in an open tuning that started on a ferry. Imagine what that would do to her. Imagine also saying to her, *And while you're at it, why don't you put a cadenza in it?*

I wrote that piece and then another. They didn't take long. He'd once told me that good work, no matter how strange, gets recognized, and I held on to those words for a while until I let them go and didn't need them anymore. If prose could change keys from paragraph to paragraph, they did so. If the strings could be retuned to make weird modalities? They did that too. They'd be shaped by surprise, surprise within the everydayness, and patterns that meant to subvert your expectations, to find the word that would saturate the one behind it, dyeing the entire passage a color I'd never seen come from me before. Art needs rebellion or else its engine won't turn, get heated.

I printed them out on a frigid winter day, arranged them out on the oak table. Light poured through the windowpane, which was so cold that it was frozen from inside.

In a year a collection called *Unbuilt Projects* would come out. I used that name because I'd always been fascinated by the gap between plans and their final executions, especially those plans that never got built. I hoped that the short fragmentary pieces of the book implied the fuller worlds of something more complete.

I wrote something I hadn't expected to write, and maybe that was why I occasionally felt severely impatient with Joni when the music ran out of her hands and into others', and she stopped buffing every note, and unforeseen chordal shifts appeared to matter less. She was trying to please some entity, but she didn't believe in that entity. She talks about it directly in some songs: "Taming the Tiger," "Lead Balloon"—the list goes on.

What I didn't understand: Nothing is made without the input of others. There is always someone who administers the push, the loving kick, *write that.* There is always some spur, some thorn. And it doesn't often happen comfortably.

He gave me a gift. *Thank you, gift.* He took me from one square to the next. He led me toward something for which I already had a gift and said, *You could do whatever you want. You could go there.*

I believe in you.

When I first heard "The Wolf That Lives in Lindsey," I thought, *There—there she is, the Joni I know.* Fingertips drumming the wood of the body, harmonics ringing like chimes, bar chords dense with minor 11th chords, shifting keys without a center. She was stretching her imagination with every line and doing the same to her listener, to those willing to make that pact with her. Joni had already prepared her listeners for alternate realms—"The Jungle Line," "Paprika Plains," the entire third side of *Don Juan's Reckless Daughter*—in ways that some felt abrasive, a betrayal to their loyalty. In this particular track, she is singing about murder, a serial killer of women, sex workers—but doing it through a tone that at first feels like coolness but is just the opposite. She is seducing herself, seducing you with beauty—why? To say that the violence isn't simply out there but possibly inside you, if the conditions are right. We are all capable of violence in a culture that doesn't care for us, not an idea that everyone is willing to sit with.

The song isn't glorifying violence. Not fetishizing it, not romanticizing it, as in the manner of a noir film, though it does have cinematic elements in its chords, which suddenly turn violent in its outro, as if her right hand is in attack mode. Not how heavy metal players once broke and set their guitars on fire but the acoustic version of destruction. She doesn't want to annihilate her instrument but is pulling out its harshest possibilities through the sound hole, to be closer to violence through noise.

In the background: Water gongs. Don Alias's congas, but sparing in their use. Chill-giving. Scampering paws ready to run up into the Hollywood Hills.

～～～

My mother died; my best friend died. Their deaths happened so close together—three months apart in 2009—that my brain didn't have the capacity to tell them apart. My mother's loss I could feel, yes, for an initial three months. She visited me in birds, rabbits, seals, even an otter in a place I never expected to find one, but once Denise died three months later, the walls between the two of them collapsed, and they became a single organism. Loss a hybrid animal. I could mourn Denise more readily because we'd become much closer in the last two years of her life. Our friendship deepened after she'd been diagnosed with stage four lung cancer—who else had I ever been so direct with about love? I told her I loved her every time I saw her. My mother, on the other hand, was harder to grieve because dementia wouldn't stop changing her. Dementia took her away from us, gave her back for a minute or so, then took her away again, which made those changes even crueler. Why had she gone back to childhood so frequently, the world that didn't include us, as if she'd been waiting her whole life to escape time? Is childhood where you inevitably go when you don't like where your life has taken you, when you're tired of having been in charge of so much? When you don't have to worry anymore about having hurt anyone, failed anyone, much less yourself? Or am I being unfair about dementia, talking about it as if she'd decided to climb up an escape hatch when she'd had enough, when, more than anything, my mother had wanted to be with us? My mother had wanted to be with us.

I tried to remember her—all the lovely things about her that those changes had obscured. Her laughter, her ability to laugh at herself, especially when my brothers and I made fun of a little trait of hers. Her eagerness to take us on half-day drives, never with any destination in mind. *Water.* From her chair she could look at the water of the bay for hours at a time and be lulled by its motion, the boats moving through it, into a state of peace. Her daily trips to the food store, which were always less about buying food than a desire to be among others, in motion. Her pride in us whenever we spoke or performed before a crowd. When the people in the seats burst into applause or laughed, especially if we made the crowd laugh. That was when she could see us as apart from herself, and that's when her spirits swelled. Her delight in getting to know someone after having decided that she didn't like that person, and the sweet relief of those old judgments sloughing away. The kindness she was often afraid to show others out of fear of being judged and hurt, but it had been there, always. As expectant as a child reaching up for her mother.

～～～

The Ghost must have watched me for days, weeks. The Ghost must have thought, *He hasn't had enough hurt. Two deaths? That's nothing. Every other person walking down the street has lost more. His hide needs to get thicker, thicker than a crocodile. Two objects out on the water don't make for a pleasing display. Two lines in a poem? Boring. No one needs another couplet. Put in a third line and you have a tercet. That's where the energy begins; that's where the wind machine starts clanking.*

Or maybe my hurt was simply an obstacle. A concrete wall where there had once been a view onto a forest. A fact that needed attending to, that stood in the way of the Ghost's ability to go deeper, to keep wandering till the old self was unrecognizable. Grief—living in proximity to someone's grief is as contagious as the flu. Grief insists there is stability, accountability. Grief is as much about losing one's old self as it is losing cherished people. The Ghost had lost enough and had spent years trying to get out from under that state of mind, and now he had to live through grief in me? Not again.

I was never going to be the person I once was, shiny and sweet as a retriever. I was never going to be new again, and maybe that was scary. Maybe everyone who had been in my life to that point was scared of me. Emotions sparking like a flooded house with the circuit breaker still on. See me burn—first the siding around the kitchen crinkles and goes black. Then the glass in the windows bubbles. The wood turning into another material entirely, not quite flesh but a substance closer to chicken.

It was so easy to ruin a long attachment through a couple of strategic actions. Make sure the gesture comes out of nowhere, outside during a heat wave in the summer, on the dead grass. Do it with a hug, with your arms holding him from behind. One gesture, one more right next to it. That was the math. That was all it took.

There must have been a thrill in tearing it all down, to know that power in oneself, even though it must have crushed him more than it did me.

Perhaps I'd walked through my life with a face that believed too much in steadiness, believed I'd glide through time without being hurt, believed in the logic of mental health to give shape to a life. What did I know? Nothing, it turned out. To walk through the world like that—to think that every need could be counted on— food, electricity, love—when there were so many people suffering close by. How much of my good fortune had depended on the acts of the suffering? I'd have been appalled by myself too if I'd had the capacity in me to see. A belief I had the right to happiness just because I'd been through too much. Too much! The person stocking cans in Wegmans had been through all that and much more by the time they were twenty-three!

You could turn a whole span of years into a mirage, and when you looked up, the land that held your house was a prairie. You could do that to a building. You could do that to a TV show. To a religion, a piece of art, a snake plant, love. Maybe it was most satisfying to do it to love. Kick it around some. A torn milk carton full of gasoline, throw the match. You didn't know there was anything there to lose until you watched it burning.

It was easier to think of him as the Ghost than it was to say *my ex*, which hooked underneath my jaw every time I said it aloud.

~~~~

When I couldn't make love work, I wrote. More short pieces: two pages, three pages, sometimes a paragraph, sometimes less—the most I could do under these circumstances, but they were one way to get to ten p.m. They first came slowly, then a little faster. They weren't as autobiographical as the first book of these I'd published, which couldn't not be about my mother's illness even when they appeared to be about something else: getting lost on a run in Palo Alto, watching from a distance as the piano of my childhood was rolled away, without ceremony, on a truck. These newer pieces were different, far away from the coordinates of my autobiography. A stranger throws lye into a man's face at a bakery one fair and sunny morning. A bulldog gets left behind at home as his human is mysteriously taken away. Someone makes it through the day by jumping repeatedly from the twenty-first-floor window of his new apartment in his imagination, thus making sure he doesn't have to carry out the act. A woman who can't abide the gentrifiers in her neighborhood picks up a seemingly benign snake before it sinks milky fangs into the skin just above her heart. Unlike the short pieces I'd written previously, which were actually poems that went all the way to the right margin, these were parables and myths. Narratives rather than inquiries. They were meant to correct those who are too ready to be seduced by lightness and hope. They were to remind us that creation promises nothing, that if we are brave enough to look past the illusions that hold our lives together, we will see that fate punishes joy, chastens any expectation of intimacy, tenderness, connection.

Did I believe any of that? I was trying desolation on for size, as they say. In some ways that state of mind was what the literary world appeared to want at that moment, a distrust of softness and warmth, which was thought to be of bad taste, the domain of the greeting card. In that way it made assumptions that its readers were likely white and straight, living comfortable lives. They needed to be shaken up—*wanted* it, in fact. No sense that the readers who reached for that book could have been living lives that were anything but orderly, lives scoured by racism, gun violence, homophobia, transphobia, mass incarceration, poverty.

At the Conference That Distrusted Softness, I stood before the crowd and read a series of these pieces thinking they were too soft, too friendly for the crowd. I got to the ten-minute mark, where I caught myself pulling away from the person I knew, as if my soul had separated from an adhesive strip with a suction sound. It wasn't me anymore; I was in a script. The script carried me along, and I was at best its delivery system. All the while, audience members looked up to me from metal seats, politeness on their faces as a way to disguise deeper feelings: *He's friendly enough, this guy, but his work? Too soft. He's using his work as a means to get us to like him. Hold up a picture of an old dog, a dog who's been separated from his human, and I bet you'll see his eyes water up.*

After the reading, one of my colleagues came up to me and gripped my arm just above the elbow. The look in his eyes suggested agitation—I steeled myself for an accusation, and even before he opened his mouth, I told myself I could take it. I'd still be standing on my own two feet on the other side of it.

"That story about the snake?" he said. "That's pretty hard on a listener. You really ought to give some consideration to that."

This was the story about the woman who had picked up the snake from the road. The story in which its fangs sank into her skin. That took no mercy at her shock. It let that shock play out in silence, as if it were saying, *This is the world as it is when we peel away our layers of illusion, all the layers we spin to protect us from truth.*

I didn't know what to say, and signed a book for the person behind him. Was his comment an insult? I walked away to my hotel room, more gratified and in awe than I should have been. The thought that I could write something that troubled another writer, someone who prided himself on his coldness! Maybe his coldness was all for show, and beneath that, he knew himself to be blessed and protected and was ashamed of his good fortune, his privilege. He needed an antidote: the clover road that ended in ashes. Or else it was just that he thought such work made it all too easy for the audience to like the performer, and thus he'd prefer to be taken into the hot red-yellow of rage, which he didn't realize was already of a piece with sentimentality and maybe even of the same cloth, even though it pretended it was made with stronger fiber. Both were too cohesive and coherent when real feeling *was* ambivalence. Feeling was multiple states stacking up on top of one another like the voicing of Joni's complicated chords.

But he wasn't lining up with what I had expected of him, and now what? When I stepped away from my work, there was a side of me that was shaken. I didn't want my words to simply be

181

the repository of hurt. I didn't want to be anguish's conductor, to carry a charge to people who'd already been suffering. I'd simply wanted to stand next to its power to show myself that it could be withstood. That was something to offer a reader too, right? If I could withstand it, you could too, which was not the same thing as saying that the conditions for that hurt should have been tolerated or enabled. I wanted to feel the current all the way down to my feet so that I'd never be wounded again.

~~~~

Maybe the hardest thing about being alone is not sharing a space with someone. It's not the conversations that you miss—you can replicate those in your head. It's the moving around the kitchen, the cooking together, watching vegetables steaming and browning as the liquid in the saucepan pops. Setting the table, cleaning up, drying, putting things back in the cabinets and drawers—the bodies don't even realize that they're in conversation, but they are. They're shadowing each other's movements, even though nobody is doing the talk.

But the voice—the voice shouldn't be diminished either. Is it harmful to go through the day when you're not using that voice, when your primary communication is through that flat box of the phone, words thumbed or pecked into a square? No wonder I sound groggy and interplanetary when I order coffee first thing in the morning. Aloneness is appealing when there are people nearby, people speaking from the other side of the house, distracting you from the project you've been asked to finish in two days. Aloneness is a good thing when you can choose it. If you've been

SONG SO WILD AND BLUE

lucky, you've known some moments in your life when you could choose it. Maybe that is the deepest occasion of good luck.

~~~~

Every life requires tests—that wasn't news to me. And if this wasn't my test, my time out in the desert, I didn't know what else was coming for me. Maybe that was why I was nurturing it as I would a philodendron, spraying it with water, fertilizing it every two weeks. I behaved as if there was something to learn about myself. For all I knew, the plant was going to die, no question about that, but look how spectacular the leaves grew. They were the size of dinner plates before some fungus blackened them in the span of a week.

Joni certainly knew what it was to be tested: through her health, her battles with the music business, difficulties with relationships, difficulties with her mother, giving up a child for adoption. She didn't appear to think tests toughened anybody up, made us stronger. She wasn't afraid to create work that sat in the bleakest condition, that felt no compulsion to transform it into light. "The Sire of Sorrow," "Last Chance Lost," "The Windfall." The dark cocoon of "The Last Time I Saw Richard." A good percentage of the songs on *Dog Eat Dog*, which I'd once undervalued, even dismissed, for what I thought of as reflexive, default desolation. Where was their polarity? The *hope and hopelessness* that spun the engines of "Hejira" and so much of her best work? In some cases, it felt like the score had already been written before she'd sat down to lay out the chords and words. There was no move to shake up the known or to look up the sleeve of the coat to describe the magenta lining inside. And this was a problem for someone whose work was dependent on second-to-second discovery, in the music, the words, even in her phrasing, which did whatever it could to intensify the pictures of her words, including wobbling her vibrato to evoke the rippling of light on the water. The standards she'd already set for herself were sterling, and when she wasn't maintaining them, it was all too evident. It was white space, music a hundred other people could have written.

Maybe, as I'd learned in other instances, she was already one step ahead of me.

~~~~

Rainy night, windy night. Subway platform, A train. Fifty-Ninth Street–Columbus Circle. By the turnstiles, four bearded young men lifted their horns and began to play Bach. Four melodies, four tones, filled the tunnel at once. My eye fixed on the tracks, on the junk down there. A little rat ran through the junk. Like everyone else on the platform, I pretended I wasn't a struck tuning fork. That's what the city wanted: obedience, detachment, emotional suppression. We were already dreaming into the thing we were on the way to. And yet something important was going on here. I knew it; I suspected the other people beside me knew it too. It was our secret. This wasn't just music but a village. Four voices in conversation, mimicking, talking back to one another. They lifted us above the trash. The one light of my train was coming up the tunnel. Soon the village would be taken down in the noise of it, but that was all right; that was a part of the pact. Perhaps the playing (and listening) wouldn't be so animated if there weren't some shared awareness of interruption. And then it occurred to me: this might not have been a village we were listening to but something nearer, inside us. It was the sound of consciousness, the song of the human brain thinking four opposing things at once.

~~~~~

I stood behind the podium at the head of the hall, thanking all the people I was supposed to thank. The dean was there, the department chair, my students, colleagues in the English department—all looking at me, actively looking, in the way that faces in a jury box look at someone on the witness stand. I was auditioning for my life, though I didn't say it like that to myself— too melodramatic. I'd had a job there, and in order to keep that job beyond my two-year visiting writer's contract, I had to show my colleagues that I was worthy of their company, the standards they'd set for themselves. I had to introduce myself again after having already known them. This meant hard faces looked even harder than they would have looked otherwise, because we'd laughed together over the last two years; we'd bumped into one another outside the men's room or by the water fountain that merely sputtered air. Were the hard faces reacting to the work I was reading, the story of the mother's car stuck in a snowbank? Maybe my reading made it all too clear that the work wasn't exactly geared toward pleasing, and the hard faces were metab- olizing that, and what was being a community member if you weren't on some level trying to ingratiate? I held those faces in my imagination without being driven by winning them over, which I might have done at any earlier point in my life. Instead, I set them free. I said no: I didn't have to control them. I gave them the permission to think about anything but me, such as how long it would take them to drive the Schuylkill Expressway at this hour and how long this performance would spiral.

Then a Q and A. Then—done. People bought books and weren't afraid of coming up to talk to me. There was nothing like a signing line stretching all the way to the back of the hall and out the doors, but that was quite all right. People weren't afraid of me, because I didn't ask deference of them. I never would have.

I climbed into my Prius with a sense of low-level satisfaction, nothing like the triumph I might have felt as a younger writer. Triumph burns off the oil too quickly, and I didn't want whatever I'd done in there to burn off just yet. I wanted the little lamp of it to keep me lit, warm. The Xanax I'd taken to get me through the presentation was just now wearing off, and I simply felt sleepy, but good sleepy. By this point, I'd moved from a city that had never felt like home, to a sky blue cottage three blocks in from the boardwalk and sea, in Asbury Park. I was trying to see if I could make new friends, build a community, find out if I wanted to put down roots. To try it out, I was house-sitting for a friend, which involved putting my furniture in a storage unit and putting off adulthood when I'd already been an adult for quite some time now, though it often felt like I was the last to know. The seventy-seven-mile drive from campus could feel endless even in the best of weather conditions, but the drive felt longer than usual tonight, the asphalt ahead of me empty. The woods were dense on either side. I'd thought of the animals that might be inside that layered mass—deer, coyote, bears. I knew they were in there, but for them it was best to stay hidden tonight, rather than poised to cross, waiting for a break in the headlights. Why was I so tired—cellularly tired? It wasn't simply that Xanax. Had I had wine? How many glasses? Every so often the tires drifted onto the rumble strip with a startling grating sound, as if the whole chassis weren't so tightly built. I turned the wheel to the left. A mile more, then I was at it again. Blink, wrench myself awake. Steering column, vibrating, shaking, as if the whole car could fly apart. Ten more miles to go, or maybe less. I felt it was ridiculous, this exhaustion. I suppose this was why rest stops were built at one time, before it was decided that they'd been put to secretive purposes.

As to what happened between where I was and where I ended up?

The weather was clear. No rain, too early in the season for snow and sleet. Midforties? Fifty? No obstacles other than that I was worn out by the night, by where my life had led me, and I'd been holding myself together for a good year, and now on my night of small triumph, my body had said, *No, enough of this fuckery.* Had the driver behind me seen my car weaving? Had the person in the passenger seat said, *Hey, that person looks like he's drunk—call 911*? Had the driver accelerated to get away from me? Or had the red brake lights of my car looked like any other car on this undertraveled four-lane highway through largely Republican Monmouth County in 2012, and this was what all catastrophes looked like before they ended up in explosion? Scorching the overpass with an ashen exclamation point that would never wear off in the sun and freezing rain.

At another point, a couple years later, I was out with my friend Elizabeth at a restaurant in Austin. I'd given a reading at the university, believed I'd enjoyed giving the reading, and though I was tired from having gotten to the airport at four thirty a.m.,

I was so happy to be out with my friend, whose company meant everything through rough times. And as I was talking, according to Elizabeth, I began opining at some length about washing machines with a tender, enthusiastic expression, though nothing had been said about washing machines all evening. My eyes were wide-open. In spite of being partially asleep, I was interested and observing. One moment I was the self I convinced myself I was in charge of, and the next? There was no seam between that state and my dreamland. When the two of us left the restaurant, I started remarking on the names of Austin apartment complexes, which are surreal anyway, but my commentary went increasingly strange as I tried to pull myself back to consciousness. I was fighting to keep my eyes open. Reportedly I didn't say anything embarrassing or offensive, but I was enjoying my friend's company and trying, as we all do, to stay alive.

When I came to this time, the car was stopped in an empty parking lot of what appeared to be a house of worship. There were trees around the perimeter. I pulled out my phone to see where I was: a synagogue, a rectangular brick structure with steps to the front door. Off a road I'd never traveled before, three towns north, in Deal. I'd missed my exit and possibly two. A Borscht Belt comedian would've known exactly what to do with my predicament. There was definitely a joke here, and still is. *Missed opportunity?* I might have written in the margins of one of my students' manuscripts. And others, not without humor, would have suggested I give some thought to conversion. I put the car in reverse, drove with extreme caution out of the lot, past a row of seedlings with their plastic tags still attached. My eyes didn't close once. The stores I passed were closed, though, the lights of their signs blazing, keeping me awake. Everyone went to bed early, as they do in a seaside town weeks away from the holidays, when people are still recovering from summer crowds months after the fact. They'd continue to recover until April, when those same crowds would start coming back with their fold-up cabanas and striped blankets.

I was feeling too spacious for the expected reactions: chest thudding, gums drying out above the upper teeth, behind my molars. Any of the body's signals of relief, chastening, or dread.

I could have been killed. Or I could have killed myself, if it's possible to have agency in blackout conditions.

It wasn't until I was in bed, duvet pulled up to my chin, eyes held open, that I realized I could have killed somebody else. All the lights were on, and I was too tired to turn them off.

Was that the wolf in me? Not the one who might have driven his car into another car, taking a mother from her children, but the delay in coming to the obvious conclusion. I'd been so long on my own that I hadn't even thought there was anyone to look out for but myself. I was my child, my father, and my grandparents all at once. My life hurt. And maybe that's what my tiredness was. I'd forgotten how to look out for others because I didn't think I'd mattered enough to wreak havoc.

~~~~

When asked for their favorite Joni song, nobody ever said, "The Wolf That Lives in Lindsey." No one gave it enough consideration to say, *Really?* Even when the discussion went solely to innovations in guitar technique, the song went unmentioned, as if it were some floating animal, untethered to the larger body of work, too dangerous to merit extended examination. When people covered it, they held back vocally, as if they were afraid of it, as if the audience wouldn't go for it, or worse, some feral energy might take over the song and get the best of the performance. No one spoke with enthusiasm of its chiming harmonics or the vocal prowess it required to sound as much wolf as human. Those leaps! And what of those sorrowful wolf voices that dovetailed so beautifully with those minor chords, so layered? "The blizzards come and go." It remained a zeroed-out spot on the Joni time line, a blackout on the long road home. Its neglect told us more about the darker side of ourselves than we cared to think about.

A CASE OF YOU

〰〰〰

JONI OPENED HER 2013 LUMINATO FESTIVAL PERFORMANCE WITH a long introduction, a string of stories, as if it were impossible to tell just one. One needed to pool into the other, so the story of honor ending in World War II poured into the relentlessness of British Columbia rain, then living with illness over the long term. There was the painter Emily Carr too—mostly she talked about Emily Carr, whose own struggles with health gave Joni the frame to talk about her own, which she hadn't done much of in her work, except through others, particularly men: Beethoven, Charles Mingus, Furry Lewis. The introduction was as much a song in itself as the song to follow. She spoke to her audience as if she hadn't been away from people, hadn't lost any social skills in all the years she'd been in bed. It was the voice of someone who loved to charm, who felt her fans' love rolling toward her in a wave, which she turned back on them but gently. She didn't always know when she was funny, which was charming. The audience laughed, and I felt her catching that reaction seconds late. Was that how humor came when she was writing lyrics? Probably so. *Gee, that was funny, wasn't it?*

I listened to the audio version on YouTube if only to hear the song. Otherwise, I'd get swept up by her gray tunic or her blond hair pretzeled on top of her head. Two verses in, I thought about all the times I'd listened to her songs, baffled, a little snowed under, not even sure I cared enough to proceed, only to come back again and again until I finally stepped aside and allowed it to enter me. This time was different. *After all this time, six years after* Shine, *this? This is all you have for us?* No dissonant chords or harmonic leaps, no approximation of a melodic line recast from verse to verse. Even the better part of the text isn't hers, as it is adapted from a passage in Carr's book *Hundreds and Thousands.* The most distinguishing characteristic is its rhyme scheme, which sounded louder to my ear than if the text had been sung. Rhyming in this case feels like a way to emphasize order, consonance—*art* in what listeners might otherwise hear as artlessness.

Artlessness? In Joni? I'm not talking about the sonic landscape behind her voice, shimmered and rumbled through the dexterity of the players. It's the text itself, which is an extended bout of sourness. Joni had done extended bouts of sourness before in "The Sire of Sorrow," "Dog Eat Dog," and "Sex Kills," but in those cases, music transformed their atmosphere. Music offered polarity. Music made sure the song wouldn't be received in one direction but several.

I never went back to "This Rain, This Rain," a song you can only access on YouTube, the way I had gone back to "Don Juan's Reckless Daughter" as a teenager, but I thought about it for years and thought about all the ways the song was about limit at its most profound. What was it like to contend with limit when it was no longer possible to teach herself how to walk again or find a new way to retune her guitar? The body has an ending, and the body will get sick. It deteriorates; we lose our flesh and bones, our eyesight and hearing, our neurons. How do you live with that fact? Do you simply go through your days ignoring it, or, if you're lucky, try to put it off as long as possible through exercise, injections, surgery? Joni had known illness all the way back to her nine-year-old self. But she'd always known how to beat it. Sheer will—or so she'd thought. What was it like to be someone who spent a life breaking out of boxes, refusing to be jammed into boxes, only to experience the body as the box again? And at this age. Seventy? No way she was going to start all over again.

If "This Rain, This Rain" is a map, she doesn't sweeten the isolation of sickness, not once. She explodes the myth of learning from adversity. She sings the grim side of the Sunshine Coast, the same place she'd loved so well from song to song on *For the Roses* and *Shine*. She tells the truth on her own terms, even if you might be put off, even if you think art should be a synonym for transfiguration. No hiding.

What, if not limit, is the destroyer of nuance?

"This Rain, This Rain" might be the darkest personal piece she's ever written, but it's prescient all the way to its marrow. It's as if she could already see the years ahead, in which she'd have to learn to walk and talk again after a brain aneurysm left her for days on the floor. But maybe those efforts require so much, they don't leave much room for the self. She was getting ego out of the way by first indulging in it. She was cleansing it out of herself, in preparation for the hardest human task.

My father parked on Northeast Fifty-Sixth Street, half-busy, half-not, not wide enough to be safe from other cars. He walked past palms and a crisp Floratam lawn, freshened by sprinklers. As usual, he walked into the front door without knocking. Said hello to one of the aides, who was feeding someone applesauce from a spoon. Looked straight at my mother, who was staring at him from a lounge chair. At a certain point, the combined smell of broth, sweat, incontinence, and electric heat coils had started to feel like home. He'd once said his daily visits to assisted living were about making sure that he was getting his money's worth, making sure our mother was being treated well, but I thought something else was going on too: this was as much routine as my mother's afternoon visits to the supermarket. He was leaving the familiarity of the condo, extending his circle of friends, talking as much to the women who worked at the facility as he did to my mother, for whom extended conversation was difficult. Words never lost their meaning, but her consciousness could shift three times over five minutes. Maybe that helped her to endure the confines of a small space where she moved between two rooms, one in which she slept, the other in which she sat all day in an armchair between two women, one of whom bickered with her.

The room was five degrees too warm, as usual. Another of the aides was heating up Campbell's soup, stirring a saucepan on the stove. What was it like for him not to know who he'd meet today? Not to know what name he'd be called by? Some days he was Bernice, the woman who worked the hypothetical cafeteria in the hypothetical basement; some days he was the handsome visitor who had just walked into her life unannounced. Other days she remembered their lives together with such accuracy that she could summon up the name of the Lighthouse Point pizzeria where our family sat around a table in 1998. Maybe it was secretly compelling to start back over again and again, when the narrative they'd built of their lives contorted who they were for each other, had gotten out of their ability to control it. To live without the weight of their disappointments and misunderstandings. To step out of themselves, their history. To hold each other's hand while Barbara, the woman who sat beside them with her magnificent hair, said derisive things about her daughter-in-law when she really meant them about my mother, whose presence made her jealous right now. My mother had the visitor by her side. Only a narcissist, even when she has dementia, is psychically attuned to those who hate her and those who don't.

My mother hated Barbara.

My father carried over a cup of Red Rose, the tea bag's paper square hanging over the edge by a string. With their old coordinates gone, they became geometry: two variables, x and y. They were ever new to each other at a time when not much else was fresh and different. The condo that they'd once shared was so big now that my father, consciously or not, stopped throwing things out. Over time the rooms filled with stuff. He didn't simply cover the surface of the dining table until there was no place to pull up a chair to eat but stacked books onto the queen-sized bed they had once shared. How many pounds did those books weigh? Did they add up to a whole person? For himself, he kept a two-foot-wide space for sleeping. Maybe the sag of the mattress made him believe he was still sharing it with her.

~~~~~

In Joni's "Furry Sings the Blues," the speaker visits Furry Lewis, the country blues guitarist. The song doesn't make it clear that she's a fan of his work or that they share an affinity for open tunings. Instead, she concentrates on the state of his Beale Street neighborhood as a way to think about the passage of time, the crumbling of Memphis's once vibrant Black music scene. It must be easier to fixate on the state of his neighborhood—boarded-up snack bars, tailors, grocery stores—than it is to keep her attention on Lewis. In 1917 he had tried to hop a moving train and, in the wake of his fall, had to have his leg amputated. For the rest of his life, he wore a prosthesis. And in the song he's propped up in bed, no dentures in his mouth, no leg. Meanwhile the legacy of redlining, segregation, and racism in all its forms, both visible and invisible, chews up the blocks around him.

At this late point in his life, Furry had been rediscovered and reclaimed by white musicians; he'd opened twice for The Rolling Stones, he'd been on *Johnny Carson*, played a bit part in a Burt Reynolds movie. He was used to famous musicians making tours of his neighborhood, stopping by to ask him to play in exchange for liquor and cigarettes. By 1976, the year of Joni's visit, he must have had enough. He must have felt invaded, a little like a sideshow, a windup. Words are exchanged between the two. "I don't like you," says Furry in the song, but the speaker doesn't do anything with that, doesn't wonder why he's put off, doesn't think, *What did I do?* Are her feelings hurt? Is she embarrassed? At that point he's a variable for everyone who's ever diminished her, and she does what people have the capacity to do when they don't have perspective: they take it personally. The speaker is trapped by her whiteness and privilege, which she acknowledges by mentioning the limo at the curb. She can't think of a way to dismantle her perspective. Instead, she sets about describing the long dismantling of the neighborhood.

But there is an untold story behind the song. Its perspective is shaped by someone who had come up against limit, especially when it comes to the body. Did it unnerve her to see Furry sitting up in his bed, disposition so sour, shaking his finger at her? Was he a glimpse into her future self? The younger musician coming into her house to pay her homage, and all she can do is mutter and scold?

As for Furry, maybe he already sensed: *This woman's hiding something, and I can't put my finger on it. She's going to make material of me. She's going to write a song, make money on my back, and not in a good way, not in a way that will honor me, just the way white people have made money destroying my neighborhood, my culture.*

In the world of the song, there are others in the room. Maybe it all would have been different if it had just been the two of them together. If neither had been performing for group approval. Who would they have been to each other? They could have talked about the guitar, the freedoms they gave themselves: Joni barring the neck with the index finger from the top down, Furry and his slide in Spanish tuning. They could have traded guitars and shown each other how they'd made the instrument their own, worked with buzz, warp, bend. How they pushed back against any other musician who tried to get them to conform.

The title of Lewis's comeback album: *Back On My Feet Again.* Not so far from the central trope of "A Case of You."

But there was too much damage between them to connect. The gap too wide to bridge. Black and white. Equals as musicians? Not on your life. Not if Furry could put a stop to it.

Furry Lewis would live five more years in his rooming house in Memphis.

He despised the song that Joni wrote about him and believed she should have paid him royalties.

~~~~~

My mother lay in a casket at the head of the largest hall in the world. It had no dividers to cordon off the space, which meant it insisted on an audience, a big one. My eye drifted to all the plush gold chairs. Who would come tonight? I looked behind me, trying not to be conspicuous. My aunt Catherine in the second row. My mother's best friend, Rita, flown down just now from Boston. My brothers beside me. Anybody else? I panicked but did my best to hide it. I concentrated on the idea of the front door, as that was something I could manage and control. I imagined someone walking by on Federal Highway. *Please, stranger, come inside for a minute. What do you need, a gift card? A ride to the other side of town? Can I buy you dinner?*

To occupy myself I started counting up the seats. Who would have this many people at their wake? You'd have to be an actor, a football star, a preacher, a cult figure. You'd have to be a Joni. The room swelled to the size of a stadium, turning the little body at the front of the room into an idea, someone who never had dreams or feelings. A grain of rice.

Dozens of people from my parents' building would come

to the funeral mass the following day, though I didn't know that yet.

My mother had died alone, as everyone I'd loved before or since had died alone, in the middle of the night, after everyone else had gone home, after having felt that turn in the room: the group's collective concentration and benevolence a thread away from impatience. And now she was alone again, her wishes not heard or attended to. She didn't want her face to be looked upon by others. She'd hated what embalming did to a person, a creepy and overly reverent approximation by someone who had never known her when she was living. She thought it was barbaric. But my father reverted to some obsolete idea of tradition when pressed with the funeral director's request. Her body would be cremated, but before that, she would have a viewing, in the manner of all of his brothers and sisters who died before him.

Why didn't I say, *But this wasn't what she wanted*? And now here I was, living with the fallout of ignoring her wishes. My mother. Terrible things can be endured if it's only for an hour. I could make it through any hour, I told myself, imagining my hand in a tank full of green water and piranhas.

Five years before, I was sitting at the kitchen table in their condo, on the most unremarkable day, on a visit home. My mother was making French toast. In the middle of stirring egg yolks and milk, she put down the whisk, looked at me as if astounded I'd shown up when I'd already been home for two days. She lay down the bread in the batter. "You knew my twin brother," she said. "You went to school with him." Nothing fell off the table or the wall. My mother's twin brother, of course, the one killed in the accident, the brother I was named for. The floor beneath my chair didn't creak, nor did the ceiling break open above me. There was love in her line of questioning—awe. She enjoyed this. "Then you lived down the street from him," she said, as if she were getting closer. She was laughing, as if delighted with herself. There had been a world that existed just out of her reach, and maybe that world was right here, in front of her. Maybe she could still catch it in her hands before it fell through her fingers. Maybe there was a game to play at the heart of it.

I made eye contact with my father. The face he gave back was primal in its fear, childlike. He'd been hiding, and he knew he'd been caught.

Hiding had been rampant in the household of my childhood. Hiding what one felt, what one liked, who one wanted to touch. The only thing that was okay was being open about what one disliked. Hiding had felt like my father's currency, and that was the economy through which we operated. Rules could be broken at every minute. Even scarier that the rules were secret, because they could change every five minutes, depending on the weather inside his head or out the window. He could be a dozen people within the span of a day. How much of that was intended and how much of that was beyond his control, I'll never know. Likely it was a mixture of both, which does not confuse me any less.

("I was a jerk," he'd said to me once, about how he'd been as a father. His voice offhand in the way that one talks about a nobody, not a tyrant. The slightest smirk while his eyes were kind. Relief poured over me like water until I felt a stab of anger, a screwdriver pointed into the skin of my chest. *You shouldn't get off so easy*, I wanted to say. *All those years you broke our hearts.*)

But in that second, hiding was protection. He was going to

keep protecting her until he couldn't. Something had changed about him in regard to his relationships with others. Had he felt it? The lightness—and terror—of seeing another human being as real. A wall had fallen down between them. The wall kept falling again and again for the rest of the years they spent together. And only then could he see himself, or start to.

And so I didn't interfere in that moment. I left it alone, as it seemed to want to be left alone.

It changed me to see that happen. You could get out of the way of yourself and begin all over again.

~~~~~

The body must have ideas of its own when it's stricken, in a state of emergency. It must know that it was only beginning to live, in spite of falling apart. It must understand something comprehensive about human life: all that struggle, after all that affection and giving and terror, and one should get—this? The unfairness. A linear narrative turning into a fragment, without resolution. So much unfinished, unfurnished. Regrets. Relationships broken, unrepaired. Love turning back on itself, with nowhere else to go.

Or does it see that humans, even the least fortunate humans, have been given so much: sunlight, plants, water? Love—at least the possibility of it.

Maybe Joni felt her nine-year-old self again when her vision blurred and she felt herself falling to the floor. Three days down there. Every muscle and nerve saying, *Left foot, right foot. Left foot again. There.* Even if she couldn't get her joints to move.

She'd been announcing the end of her career for years. She'd been saying goodbye to her dedicated listeners since "River." Goodbyes are coded into the DNA of her songs, all the way back to the first songs, where she is thinking about relationships, places, a hallowed Earth with good air and good water. But to touch the membrane of one's almost death with such intimacy, without shuddering. Or not to feel anything at all: a zeroed-out spot, a lyric space. A poem detached from all contexts.

The world feels brand-new from down on the floor.

~~~~~

It was four p.m., an hour before the wildlife refuge locked the front gate. The humidity so thick, it smeared the air. My father and I walked among bald cypress, moss, pileated woodpeckers, herons, bugs. It was ours; we were all alone, as if it had always been built with us in mind, the boardwalk a structure built to contain and take us forward. Maybe that was all we ever needed, a chute to hold us together. It wasn't a place we were accustomed to but the closest thing to wilderness in ninety miles. What was wilderness anymore? So many humans spent their lives trying to cut it away from themselves. If just a piece of the world looked untouched, humans made sure to find a way to put their hands on it.

My father couldn't resist being the good pupil for me, a role I'd never seen him take to so keenly before. He was stepping out of the expectation that he had to do something, produce, to justify his time on earth. For the better part of his life, he couldn't go on a trip without the desire to turn around, thinking he was wasting time, which might have been the only thing worse than wasting money, though to him they were interrelated. We'd once taken a

1,200-mile road trip from Cherry Hill to Miami Beach only to turn around for home as soon as we reached the bleached towers of Collins Avenue, my brothers and I crying silently in frustration, bewilderment. Why was he missing mountains now, and why were we changing course, heading north without warning or any plan to Gatlinburg, Tennessee?

This walk took some will, a decision to say no to his habits when he'd long been so set in his ways.

Look how well-behaved I am, his gestures seemed to say. *Look at me stopping to enjoy the plants, the cardinal landing on that cypress knee before taking off. You had no idea I could be this person. You're just waiting for me to say the wrong thing, and so I say the wrong thing. Not this time. There's always a lot more of me to know.*

At the end of the walk stood a sign with an emblem and a paragraph about an alligator. A ranger in a crisp beige shirt walked out of a squat building, a smell of air-conditioning still about her, an expression that suggested that she both liked and wanted something of us. She asked if she could take our picture, and before I could reply, she was standing too close, reaching for the phone I held in my hand. Maybe she saw some atmosphere around us we couldn't possibly see, felt the down-deep knowledge that this was an occasion to mark. Maybe she saw that our ease with each other was something rare, and this walk would probably never happen again—our last walk. In the picture, I'm placing my hand on his back; I'm standing behind him, as if I'm his guardian, as if he's relying on my assistance when he's just walked over a mile on his own. He doesn't smile the way he smiles when he's the sole subject. Instead, he looks as if he's claiming his character, putting a stake in himself, as if he senses the photo's making for a situation in which the two of us are to compete. The expression in his eyes is part exposed, part hard, always an in-between face when he's photographed with another. *Don't go thinking I'm an old man.* He was already putting himself in the viewer's position, and he wasn't ready to give up his side of the story.

~~~~

At the Brooklyn coffee place with the open front doors, I walked up to the counter only to feel a presence behind me, too close, a cloud of inchoate feeling. Had I stepped in front of another person? An older guy in a navy peacoat came out of nowhere, an intractable expectation on his face. "Did I step in front of you?" I said.

"You're older," he said. "You can go first."

"No, go ahead, sir." I gestured forward with my hand. "Really."

"You're the older one," he said, angry now.

"I'm older," I replied.

The voice out of my mouth was weary, more shaken than I'd expected. I'd just taken a walk to Red Hook and was moving toward home on Court Street. The day had come with lightness. It wasn't so much that he'd turned human exchange into a matter of competition. It was a reading of my age—from what? The surgical mask over the lower half of my face? I *wasn't* older, but that was beside the point.

He'd believed I'd been patronizing him, and now it was his turn to patronize me.

Then he stepped in front of me to demonstrate that he'd already ordered, and picked up his drink from the counter.

I walked home, still unnerved, diminished, but tried to push it down. The day was still good. Why care about some guy who read *older* as *weaker*? What had he seen that I hadn't seen? I'd lost control of something, not just of that exchange but something more ineffable. No one needs reminders that for some, the idea of a shelf life pervades everything. *What a shitty way to live*, I thought, looking for the ending in everything and everyone, the very machine that pushes capital along, the gears that stoke and ruin people. But it was also a reminder that someone's perception of me was out of my hands. He had doled out a curse. I hadn't had as much time as I'd wanted to think.

If I were a dog, I'd have thrown back my head and howled till all the hurt came out of me.

~~~~

On his last trip out in the world, my father and I walked into his favorite restaurant in Lighthouse Point. Instantly the staff behind the salad counter straightened their backs. They looked alert, their faces tender, as if they hadn't known they'd missed his daily rapport until they saw him again, his face inquisitive and baffled. How long had it been since he'd last walked through those doors—two-and-a-half months? They did their best to make him feel welcome without making too much of a fuss. They knew something was different beyond the fact that he weighed a little less and walked to his usual booth with tentative steps rather than his usual swing. They didn't know that he'd just left hospice care for a second time and would go back again next week. That's the kind of news you can't even say to yourself.

We were no longer operating under the assumption that life, beyond the hour in front of us, was a race to be won.

He ordered salmon when he meant to order chicken, but he didn't feel compelled to change it. The sun was so intense through the plate glass windows that the two of us all but disappeared in the glare of it. A hanging pot of inch plant turned in the draft of the air conditioner. "Look at you," I said to him. "You're alive. What do you have to say about that?" And I wasn't simply commenting on how he looked, though he did look good, with his thick, clean hair, his striped green polo shirt. I was thinking about the fact that this moment made all routines and habits look absurd. He took no starting point for granted, and thus everything in front of us felt both strange and wonderful, from the spoons and forks and cups that called us to drink and eat, to the arrangement of the words on the menu. The various fonts. The graphics. A server bringing a hot meal on a plate? Amazing. The kindness in her face, her willingness to laugh at our jokes even when they were funnier to ourselves than they were to her. Even more amazing.

No one wanted to live more than he did, though he didn't give himself permission to enjoy very much of it. Pain justified a life, a lesson he'd taken in before he could even conceive of it as a lesson.

Other than when he went out dancing. If he'd had a choice in the matter, he'd have gone out that way, somebody he didn't yet know in his arms, his feet in the air as much as they made contact with the floor.

But today limit was outside this space, nowhere in sight. To sit here together was enough. Thanking the moment in front of us.

In three months he'd be gone. He, like my mother, would

also leave in the early hours of the morning, when none of us were around.

~~~~~

At the end of "Furry Sings the Blues," Joni sings of the dancers of the past, consigned to a culture that's being erased in front of her eyes. At the end of "Goodbye Pork Pie Hat," she sings of dancers again, but this time they're "babies," a sign of the future, the mark of the generations to come, so far ahead that we don't even have the capacity to imagine them into being. When I thought of it, dance is central to so many Joni songs, both in the foreground and background: "Cotton Avenue," "Edith and the Kingpin," "Help Me," "Dancin' Clown," "Come In From The Cold," "In France They Kiss on Main Street," "The Crazy Cries of Love," "Night of the Iguana," "Coyote" . . . And dance is never a placeholder for joy but a position toward the body, expressed through phrases, cadences, repetition. Timekeeping. The pressure plate where music originates.

Movement against limit.

To be on one's feet.

It took me years to see that for Joni, dancing was never simply about having a good time.

STAY IN TOUCH

～～～～

JONI'S SEVENTY-FIFTH BIRTHDAY CELEBRATION: NOVEMBER 2018.
Thirteen performers. Not out in nature, with the breeze blowing
between rows, but inside. An iconic space: the Dorothy Chandler
Pavilion, the venue she'd played as part of the *Court and Spark*
tour in March 1974. The first tribute she attended in the wake of
her brain aneurysm.

The sparsity of facts around her time away had suggested
that her condition had been dire. Because of that, I'd never expected to see or hear from her again, which felt like a low-level
extended mourning, even though she'd already made it clear years
before that it was time to retreat. I'd wanted her to be comfortable. Wanted her to be home. Wanted her restless, compulsively
creative mind to find engagement, an outlet, some contact with a
vital stream in at least some of its depths. Wanted her to have time
with friends, family, cats, and dogs if that was what she wanted
of some of her days. Wanted her to have good help, people who
both cared about her and what she'd meant to others. Wanted her

to have opportunities for surprise, the unexpected. Wanted her to dress up in the clothes she'd always loved. Sunlight on her face, birdsong, plants and trees, a view—those as well. Music? Maybe that could matter less now. She'd done enough. How does a life force negotiate with limitation? That was a question that absorbed me every time I listened to her, thought about her. Not a day went by when I didn't go to Google for news of her, usually coming up with nothing; at best a brief, vague report, either blandly optimistic or the opposite, and never in-between, the place where the truth lived.

I couldn't even begin to picture the worst scenario: that she was agitated, in physical pain, in some existential state where the seam between night and day didn't matter at all. Not even in the home she loved but in some facility. Like my mother near her end.

But now here she was, back again after having taught herself, with the help of her physical therapists, to speak again, walk again. Teaching herself to walk a third time! Three years out of the public eye. How had she filled that time? These days the press made a big deal out of every sighting of her, whether it was at a deli on Beverly Glen Boulevard, a brief venture in Bel-Air, or in the audience of another performer's concert up in Santa Barbara.

And now I watched her return unfold, not in person or in real time but on a screen, on YouTube.

~~~~~

Some of the performers had been a part of earlier tribute concerts and recordings, but there was a new crop this time around. Black, brown, queer performers. Los Lobos, Chaka Khan, Seal, Rufus Wainwright, Brandi Carlile. This lineup felt truer to what her music actually is. It has been fertilized by multiple sources, always. She'd never been another Peter, Paul and Mary. Maybe the audience would need to be reminded in perpetuity that she wasn't only a folk musician. Or maybe all that would change once her earliest fan base was gone, all those people who had come of age along with *Song to a Seagull*.

Beside me on the sofa sat a short stack of student manuscripts. I'd been marking them up since two p.m., increasingly worried I'd started sounding like a mechanical puppet. It seemed to me that all I ever did as a teacher anymore was to say, *Sensory language?* Everything I read felt too abstract and brainy. My students needed to be in touch with their bodies. But there had to be fresher, more evolved ways to ask for such a thing. It occurred to me that I was asking it as much for myself. What did I hear right now, beyond the frame of the music that came through the laptop? The deep rumble of the BQE two blocks away, the bells of Our Lady of Lebanon. I needed to be pulled back to my body too—not just once but all day, on the hour, which was maybe the reason for those bells in the first place. I heard those bells in my ears. The sound vibrated my eardrums. I moved through the world as a body, and one day the people who loved me would no longer be able to see and teach me. And so I needed God, a church, a community to help me process that. Was that it? Maybe music and dance were more necessary now because of all the time we spent on screens, all the screen selves ready to fly out ahead of us. It felt impossible to call them back sometimes. Who are you out there? What's your name? I'm not sure I'm here.

~~~~

By now Joni tribute concerts were legion, practically a regular feature of everyday life, whether they took place in major concert halls, in small-town coffee shops, or online. If one wasn't on the books for next month, one was coming soon if you were willing to travel, or so it seemed. A single idea shapes the need for them: How do we get Joni to stay with us, to write more songs, to make more music? By showing her that we love her. There is so much to sing against and defy, especially for those who have stuck around, been loyal to her through various changes. Years of casual dismissal, years of pressure from record industry executives, years of indifference, if not downright hostility, from music reviewers, especially men. People saying she'd done nothing listenable since *Blue*, people saying she never should have taken the jazz turn, never should have taken the rock turn, the turn to art song, synthesizers, sampling, rhythmic experimentation, the orchestral remake. *Where are the melodies? Why does this one only use the tightest cluster of tones?* An artist who knew how to squander every single one of her talents over time, and when she did try to sound like a former Joni—say on *Night Ride Home* or *Turbulent Indigo*—well, even that wasn't good enough for some people. A quality was always lacking. Youth. A high, clear soprano. Humans need to feel like the boss of what they love, especially when they cherish something.

Joni bore the scars of being loved too much, which is always predicated on a turn: *You've disappointed me. You're pretentious.* Or: *You're not the genius I thought you were; you tricked me into thinking you were immortal. You were always human. Prone to kitsch, obviousness, and bougie taste just like every other living, breathing person.* Once she ascended, she started to fall. Romantics meet the same fate. The hammers, the boards, and the nails.

Unlike Joni, nobody felt the necessity to protect and defend Bob Dylan. There is no sense that people will stop listening to his music, or that it will no longer be covered or find new ways to be interpreted. He has never sought connection with us. He couldn't care less if you think he's sleepwalking through this phase or if "Murder Most Foul" is so long that it makes your teeth hurt. This is central to his relationship with his audience, while Joni wants to touch your nerves. She doesn't mind if you flinch but hopes she soothes you in the process. She wants to sit across from you on the other side of the table. She wants to tell you what happened when she walked into the room the other night, surging with feeling and ideas, before she burns out like a light bulb.

When the first tribute was broadcast back in the year 2000 on a cable network, there was no way to review it on YouTube, which would come five years later. Full attention had to be paid to it; psychic muscles had to be at heightened alert and made porous, or individual moments wouldn't be retained. They'd fly up into the ether. It came at a moment when she'd come to the edge of being forgotten, when no one admitted how much those songs meant to them. Every participant a star, mainstream. Not just music people but other celebrities too. Goldie Hawn, Susan Sarandon—*right up front.* Cameras panned to their faces for their reactions, which were inevitably ecstatic. How had I not conceived that Joni's songs could be part of the lives of movie stars? Goldie Hawn singing

"This Flight Tonight" to Kurt Russell at two thirty a.m. and thinking about the desert outside Las Vegas.

Cyndi Lauper sang, James Taylor sang. Eleven others, all white people except for two. But all these individual performances, while well intended, had only been preparing us for the full Joni. They could at best be acolytes. She walked out onstage in a fog-colored gown to show everyone that nobody did Joni like Joni; no one could top her. Even if she was wearing a gown, even if she was singing "Both Sides Now" to the accompaniment of strings, brass, and woodwinds. She closed her eyes and emphasized her phrasing with her hands as if she'd never relied on a piano or guitar as a prop. She made sure to open up that wrenching break before "at all." She put more pressure on the final refrain but not too much. When she reached the ending, the audience rose, joy crashing the stage. *Now do you know?* the applause seemed to say. *Now do you see that we love you?* Gratitude lit her face, but her eyes looked flustered, vexed. The words *thank you* didn't come easily at this point, and she couldn't complete her sentences without pauses—she reached out to Susan Sarandon for help. She'd lost control of something, a legacy. She felt the audience's power over her. Maybe in the volume of applause, she'd heard an ending, and who would want to be told, *You are full, complete now*? What living being would want a stake driven through her? *You stop changing and mattering from this point on.*

And so began the ongoing goodbye.

She was contending with the gap between her own story of underappreciation and this extended love and glory—she had to be. To feel the truth of one's story taken from oneself: it is far easier to hold on to the narrative of the neglected. There is control in that stance, even if you have to metabolize and negotiate it. But to know that one is loved deep down, even if that is fleeting? You have to let go and see what happens, see the open farms and water streaming beneath the basket. The top of your head is hot. You're lifted out of the self you knew, which is not always the most comfortable balloon. What if it crashes: Icarus with melting wings?

~~~~

Tight place above my ears, tightness at my ankles, crossed in awkwardness and tucked beneath my chair. My posture said I didn't like the way the paragraph was coming together, and once again my body knew before my conscious mind knew. An obstacle between inspiration and execution that translates as *effort* on the page, which is another way to say showing off, trying too hard, calling attention to myself, rather than stepping aside, allowing sound itself to transmute idea and feeling. A hurrying-through, a desire to reach the finish line before the banner dissolves, in order to feel satisfaction, completion, an ownership. Reverence for humility, where is it? *I don't know life at all.* The purity. But this arrival necessitated listening to my body first. Sensory description—it was always more than embellishment for embellishment's sake. The body as pressure plate, as first teacher. I put the letter to my student aside and clicked the arrow to go back to the concert.

Was it still a tribute when multiple tributes had transpired? Back in Dorothy Chandler, the stakes were higher. We never thought she'd be well enough to leave home, but there she was in the front row, dressed in red, lips lined in red. A smile with enough light in it to destroy a concert hall.

In the wake of extremity, humans need comfort. And

mythmaking develops in the face of death, as a response to it, as Karen Armstrong offers. What else is myth but an attempt to evoke timelessness? To assure ourselves that chronological time isn't the scouring force that it appears to be, but only one way to make sense of the clock. Past, present, and future at once. Yes, life-shaping events happen in the past, but they happen once again as we summon them up with others.

What was holding such an event together? What were we celebrating? Joni, for sure—*she lived*! But the night was just as much about the audience and what it valued, as embodied by her songs. The idea that our lives, upon close examination, are beautiful, even in chaos and suffering, maybe especially so. The idea that everyday moments are inevitably shadowed with complex, simultaneous feeling. The idea that oppositions are the source from which energy springs. Doubt not as the enemy of faith but its closest friend, no less profound than the work of the Gnostic Gospels or the long poems of William Blake.

To be here, whether in person or online, was to make contact with our psychic materials. To be potentially extraordinary when your way of seeing had been dismissed and shrugged off. To put faith in the notion of retuning yourself, others. To gather multiple versions of oneself in one room, where they could sit around a table in some version of okayness. Think: the third-person multiverse of *The Hissing of Summer Lawns*, which one could read as a Joni Hall of Fame, all the different personae she inhabits.

The energy of the group was mysterious, joyful, bright. Though it didn't look or feel like church, it was church in its fullest sense. Patterns were being attended to. The foregrounding of "hits" by an artist never known for her hits, the inclusion of lesser-known songs, ideally from later, underappreciated albums. Any recognition that Joni was always at heart an experimentalist, an artist wary of pleasing the crowd.

And here's the contradiction: the liturgy always finished with a sing-along, usually either "Big Yellow Taxi" or "The Circle Game," which puts the night squarely in the tradition of folk music, the form that Joni has hurried from her entire artistic life. Some have tricked themselves into thinking they've been participating in one person's story, but Joni's music has always been the music of the people, of community. The drama of talking and listening has always been of the highest value. All along she's given us the terms of a life—a suit—to step into and inhabit. She's never been singing about herself.

You need to step out of yourself in order to be open to that.

~~~~~

Glen Hansard, the third performer of the night, could have under-played "Coyote" in the manner of Joni's performance on *Hejira*, which is somehow emotional without sounding emotional. He could have turned all the *he* pronouns to *she*, converting the song into an awkward statement of heterosexuality, reinscribing expected categories. Other male singers have done that with Joni songs over the years, only to fail, only to miss the whole point of a Joni song, which is to make discoveries about oneself, on the level of the line, in multiple ways.

But it was a more complicated era, and Hansard knew that it's always been a song about gender, more authentic expressions of roles, and he ran with that. In Joni's version, the coyote seems to be drawn to the speaker as much as he's drawn to others. The speaker's attitude throughout is to insist on her own freedom, to look at the coyote with curiosity, but nothing more than that. In Hansard's version, the rhythm is allowed to explode. Restraint is the last thing he's interested in. His speaker stumbles upon a bewildering predicament. To be the object of another man's desire: it asks of him a physical response that he might not be ready for, not without awkwardness or humiliation. Perhaps the emotion in the delivery is the anticipation of those emotions, the hunch that any touch must be paid for a hundredfold. And what is next? How does one continue to be a hitcher, free from attachment, when one encounters explosive feelings? What do you do with the words *I want you* when nothing about your self-conception until now has prepared you for such a thing?

A man dancing with another man at a country roadhouse, not masking his frustration that the coyote who's been drawn to him is simultaneously drawn to random women. The situation feels more chaotic than the original. I wondered if he was going to maintain the emotional intensity or merely begin to phone it in, fall into a script when he started thinking too much about the listener, the prospect of exposing too much of himself in all the ways that some are too threatened to hear. No, he was right there. Traveling inside the vein of it.

Who would I have been as a young person if I'd had access to this possibility in my songwriting and performances? If I'd known others would even listen without correcting it out of me, or worse, threatening me with violence? Would I have stayed in music? Imagine having access to the kind of imaginative fire that had rein to touch whatever it needed to touch. The energy that went into pronouns, turning them inside out, obscuring them, trying to navigate around them, pretending they were soft and malleable when they had all the solidity of poured concrete markers. What songwriter would want every song to be directed to an unidentified *you*, which only offers limited options, a rant ("You've got a lot of nerve") or intimacy ("You taste so bitter and so sweet")? The limited options had felt like floodlights when all I had wanted to do was hide. Those were years when to say *gay* simplified you to sex, a lexicon of practices, in which the only story was desire—desire squelched, rubbed out, punished. And though I could put the effort of hiding into how I lived, I couldn't do that to my music any more than I could do that to a child. I couldn't conceive of being a father back then, but the closest thing that came to a child was my music. A field of energy that went on ahead of me, without me. The future.

And now you might be thinking, *Why didn't you retune yourself? Why weren't you a Joni, emboldened and on fire against the structures that oppressed you? Where was the lion in you to defy it all?* I'm thinking that too, alongside you. To do that risked losing any love I had in my life, which didn't feel all that stable at the time. Love that I'd always assumed was unconditional felt anything but. By that I'm talking about those closest to me, all I had. And to lose love of any sort? I couldn't bear it. I couldn't conceive of any life on the other side of that divide. Always the sense of saying the wrong thing and being up on the high wire. Hiding drains the life out of a person. It makes you stupid, desensitized. Unworthy of an original, life-giving thought, even though you forget you're hiding when you've been doing it so long. You think, *This isn't extinguishing my cells. This isn't killing me.*

Maybe this was why the gender dramas at the heart of "Coyote" went completely over my head for so long. It was easier to think that the hitcher and coyote were just doing what heterosexuals always did with their jealousies and baiting, which seemed as comprehensible to me as the late-night language of frogs. What did I know about love when I was still tasked with getting to know my body and its urges and reconcile them to an inscrutable social world? The social world, whatever that was, that didn't have a place for me unless I was willing to force myself into a category, which might as well have been another word for *collar*. What fell away was the song, the magnificent song in all its layers and dimensions. I listened to it as a song about an actual coyote, and when I thought about it running through the whisker wheat, I only saw myself running, untethered to any other creature. Alone, but not with pity. I refused to feel sorry for myself. My situation was too extreme for that. It required too much attention to everyday survival to be a matter of feelings.

~~~~~

The transition from songwriting to fiction: Deep down under my skin, I knew it wasn't as far as it seemed. Novels and short stories lived on the other side of the room, though some would say, *Oh no*, and offer their pronouncements. I proceeded from my gut and knew. In my earliest stories, I was interested in evoking atmosphere first. To my mind, atmosphere preceded meaning and was fed by an attention to description and sound. How was that any different from a song? The trick was to make a long song in which clusters of words implied the notes. That seemed to be a good thing, especially when I didn't have to worry about the vagaries of pitch, the condition of the instrument I was playing and how it responded to the acoustics and humidity. My health. You cannot sing with a pattern of recurrent sore throats unless you're prepared to make a hero of yourself, to sacrifice the future of your instrument for nodules: little doors on the linings of your throat. I was sick of worrying about my health, afraid of getting colds and sinus infections, which might as well be death to the singer.

I didn't want scraping worry to be my ongoing psychic terrain. *Enough*, in this case, felt lifesaving. And I was in awe of musicians who could manage that.

I was sneaky about this shift in my identity. I let it happen over a long period of time—years? I started working on books that wanted to be songs. Unlike music, the audience for writing was small. I wasn't being charged with standing in front of an audience and laying myself bare—or so I thought at the time. Laying myself bare was easier to do when it involved a stranger whom I'd likely never see. Someone I'd never see turn the page while they were riding the subway or perched on the edge of a hill, looking out at a bay.

I was in my living room sofa one morning before seven. The sky was so red that it called on me to record it. It wouldn't last. Within seconds it would be the generalized gray of laundry water, which is exactly how it played out. I picked up *Lawnboy*, my first book, again. I'd been paging through its opening chapters the night before. The voice in that work? He wasn't me any more than a recording of my younger speaking voice was me. As soon as that voice went out in the world, it belonged to the reader, who made their own experience out of it. It was a relief when the work escaped me. A reader always knew my work better than I did, which was why I wouldn't have found satisfaction if my words had never traveled farther than my hard drive or the cloud.

And yet that book's narrator did find love with someone who happened to be a doctor, happened to love plants and water, happened to find love again after a great loss. What did that book know about what was to come that I couldn't yet see?

In that long period before the pandemic, when in-person readings were more frequent, I was standing on the stage of a college theater in a rural corner of New Jersey at the Q and A portion of the night. I'd just published *The Narrow Door*, a book about grieving Denise's death from cancer, and readers and reviewers had taken it in in ways I'd never imagined for my work. I'd thought it was going to empty me to read aloud from it night after night. Instead, I loved getting the chance to bring her back among others, the light in her transforming people's faces. The conversations afterward too—the audience members' questions, the challenge of meeting them with a response that was casual and down-to-earth but managed to invite them to think and wonder. "What is the purpose of what you do?" came a voice from the back row of the room. Several exchanges had come before that question, all very seamless and relaxed. I had everyone's attention in a way that made me take it for granted—so far was I from the person I'd been once, a tad on the spectrum, all halting syntax and pushing back against stage fright, which always came on without reason, no warning. And here I was now without a ready reply for him. He held the power in the room at that moment, and he knew it, but there was nothing overtly aggressive about his face and voice. Unlike me, he'd grown up in the age of branding, social media, and influencers, and he didn't see his question as invasive or impossible. I thought of telling him I wanted to write the kind of work that Joni wrote, which was work that never emptied out, work that kept offering up insights on a daily basis after I'd known those songs for decades, suggesting something about the endlessness inside us, inside creation. But what I really wanted to say had something to do with love. Not the manic exhilaration of Joni's "Underneath the Streetlight" but something harder, more inscrutable, both involving eros and transcending the body at once. Love without control of its object. Love as walking through a door into space and finding not so much a floor or a ceiling but a floating. No horror, but a space that took down the walls between past, present, and future, or old age, middle age, and youth, or, better yet, you and me. You and me. I looked at everyone in that room and knew that we would die. But to say such a thing would be like coming out all over again in a way that made the *I am gay* from my past look easy. In a better world I'd be able to sing it, which would have captured all the layers at the same time. But I needed a larger field than a song. I needed acreage. At this moment I would have rather had the song.

Instead, I said, "I think it's time to call it a night," but I said it in such a way that my evasion made people laugh, and maybe laughter was the most efficient dissolver of walls. It felt a little like trying to end a song that refused to end, the dwindling notes of the outro still audible even after I'd shut off the lights and zipped up my jacket, on my way out the door.

JERICHO

~~~~~

A LITTLE ON THE EARLY SIDE FOR LUNCH. IF THERE WERE OTHERS somewhere in the restaurant, we couldn't hear their voices—neither of us needed to strain to talk or hear. There were plants—bromeliads, dracaena, philodendrons, staghorn ferns—pots hanging from the ceiling and pots clustered on the floor. Moisture in the air that collapsed the border between inside and out. The walls, from what I could see of them, were painted deep gold: mustard. Open glass to the garden, more plants, on the verge of crowding one another out, but birds dipped in and out of red and yellow throats, extracting insects and pollen. *Don Juan's Reckless Daughter* played on the sound system.

"Do you hear that?" I tilted my head in the direction of a speaker, which wasn't there once I looked up to find it.

Joni smiled in a way that said, *Of course*—she seemed to know it had been playing minutes before I heard it, but that was all right. She wasn't chastising me for being late to the party.

We resumed our conversation, which had little to do with

music. As for its content? All I can say is that it wasn't about the complicated melody of "Jericho." Wasn't about what it had been like to refresh a song that was older than the others on the record, a song that had already been introduced through a live version on *Miles of Aisles*. I didn't ask her what it had been like to hold her ground as a guitarist and vocalist when she could have been pushed around by Jaco Pastorius's bass, with its low and fat notes, pooling in space, but never concentrated enough to *anchor*. Didn't ask her what it had been like to sing such a song of belief after she'd been through a sequence of rough and public breakups. The content of our conversation—it wasn't small talk. Neither of us had a clue as to how to do small talk. Sit down with either of us, and before you knew it, you were pulled into some story of love and death and time. What mattered was the ease of our talking. We were all right with the inevitable silences, which told me she liked being exactly where she was. The look on her face—it didn't ask too much of me. Its steady presence didn't dominate me or cause me to flick my eyes away. It received me. At some point it occurred to me that it was the kind of face I'd like to give to my students and strangers, a face that wanted them to feel taken care of. Not the kind of face that said, *I own you; I'm better than you.* It wanted to draw out the best of me, even though she wasn't afraid of calling me on my bullshit. The proof came in a close attention to the songs: "A Strange Boy," "Borderline," "Nothing Can Be Done," "Lead Balloon."

How deep had I been in the conversation when I knew it was a dream? I've had good dreams in my past in which I realized I was dreaming, and that realization broke like a wave through a lake. The boat I was on toppled over, and I was gripping the side.

It felt like I'd been tricked, or that I'd tricked myself too readily into something that I'd wanted. From then on out, the subject of the dream was lack, diminishment, a brute joke about desire, a taunt. A marker of my own greed. *Cruel optimism*, as Lauren Berlant would call it. But this was different. I didn't feel the need to tear myself out of the dream, but I bobbed in its currents, surprised I had it in me to give up control when something compelled me—especially when a person compelled me. As if so much good fortune must be hurried away from, could be more than I could handle without ruining. As if conflict were infinitely more compelling than stillness, all any human being should expect. For what else was there to distract us from time, change, the perils of our mortal lot?

Oh, what do I mean, *mortal lot*? *Bullshit.*

We die. That's it. We die, and we lose the world we know and love. The people too. Maybe that's the hardest thing.

And there she was, holding me in that awareness. Together. As if inside a circle, a ring of soft fire.

And to break open that ring would be to agree that I was alone, on my own, not someone who had come to recognize that his sense of self was interdependent. Was infused by others, so many more than I could name.

It took so long to recognize the most obvious thing.

And when I opened my eyes, my whole body was in a state of calm, as close to calm as a person could get. I didn't leap out of bed as I usually did, pushed forward by the possibility of making coffee or texting my Wordle grid to Jude, but stayed there alone, but not quite. I possibly had a smile on my face. Not just for the absurdity of a love that played out so neatly in a dream, without any notes of conflict, but for the fact that I could still believe it, hold on to it, cherish it, the two different realities rhyming together. I thought if I moved, the movement would vaporize both the dream and my meditation around the dream, so I lay still longer than I would have under any other circumstance, not even bothering to throw on an extra blanket when the temperature fell inside or when the wind flexed the glass in the window as if it wanted to pop it right out of its frame and bring the outside into the room.

SHINE

~~~

IN 2022 A SEVENTY-EIGHT-YEAR-OLD WOMAN FROM LOS ANGELES sat on the stage of the Newport Folk Festival, looking out at all the faces in the crowd. Beyond them the view didn't look like what she'd remembered, but then again nothing looked much the same seven years after a brain aneurysm. Last time she was there, the festival was closer to the center of town, surrounded by a fence. The concert was all about the fence behind her, and she hated fences. The pen of it had raised the temperature of the crowd, intensified rivalries, performer to performer, performer to audience. On her first visit, a young fan asked her in awe, with flushed face, if her name was Joni Mitchell, and all Joni could do was bolt, running out into the hot streets of town. She couldn't imagine feeling anything close to that out here beside the bay, with all that sky in sight, pennants snapping, sailboats, the wires of the suspension bridge gleaming. No fences here, and she felt her throat opening up like a rose. Brandi Carlile had told her Newport was one of the most beautiful places to perform, and now she knew why she was here. Sun on her arms, both warm and cool at once. Breeze on her face, salt air—it was that moment when the summer sun was climbing toward its peak, as if August and its endings were far away. Nothing gold can stay? She chose to differ.

And the faces in the crowd, their screaming, hands in the air! Joy. They behaved as if they were seeing Jesus but without any of the complicated feelings about Jesus—Jesus in the form of an older woman with glasses and blond braids. And maybe that's why she'd said yes to Brandi's plan to bring her back onto the stage as a surprise guest. The part of her that was a joker, a trickster— people always missed that about her. Always missing the mischief in her songs, always looking past how much she liked to laugh, as if she'd always been the writer of one kind of song, the song that tore your heart, the song you listened to alone late at night when the worst things had happened: your mother died, you lost your boyfriend when you said the wrong thing, or you got news that your best friend, the person you'd talked to every day since you were eighteen, had died on the way home from the office park in a car accident, and it was your task to go to her apartment and pick up her dog.

No one would ever capture the totality of Joni, but she was happy to be there, happy to be playing her first full concert in twenty-two years. Love poured toward her like one wave after the next, refreshing her in the heat, and she was proud she could take it in, unlike that younger self of hers who had been impelled to run and hide. If only she could bring her younger self on the stage and make her sit beside her and teach her how to take it. Whoever said it was easy to be loved?

But as the performance got underway, she already felt narratives spinning around her, little tropical storms on the weather map. There was no stopping those tropical storms. And now some of them might bypass her and lay into Brandi, the person who pulled her toward new friendships with younger musicians, who assured her that her songs were just as relevant today, who promised to take her on her boat through British Columbia's Malibu Rapids once she felt well enough to do so. They'd say Brandi was using her to bolster her own reputation or trotting her out like some circus tiger in front of the crowd. They'd accuse her of gushing on the stage. They'd say she was out of her league and was too self-pleased to see it, that she was nowhere near the caliber of Joni as an artist. The ugliest things. But there was no way you could be a musician, especially a woman musician, a *lesbian*, without being in some relationship to the ugly things. Brandi could take it, as Joni herself had learned to take it over the years—though that didn't mean it didn't scour and scrape. Whenever Joni had let the bad reviews inside, she'd wanted to stop playing—every Top 40 song from a passing car sounded either excruciating or boring. Whenever she'd refused to read anything about her, she missed out on the good words and couldn't quite believe it when someone said she'd changed their lives. She'd changed lives. That was a hard thing to hear when the intimacy only poured in one direction.

She wasn't good at math. She couldn't learn Cotten picking from Pete Seeger's *The Folksinger's Guitar Guide* without adapting it to her thumb. She couldn't read music or even the names of the chords she played, and she often put books aside after she'd gotten all she'd needed from them, but the one thing she had was a compass inside her. A compass wasn't *out there*. Rather, it had everything to do with her body, her senses, which told her what to walk away from, which chord progression to be excited by, which person in the room was a phony, and which drummer knew how to parcel out the complexities in her songs. The senses, of course, could get her into trouble—it wasn't so easy. They could make her walk away from any situation before it had the chance to settle into its terms. They could drive her to leave every relationship for the snap of freshness and adventure, that drunk-in-love feeling. They could lead her to try on a new style before the old style had borne its fruits, always desperate to try the next thing. Running and tripping through a life, getting up again. Jung said as much.

But without that compass, she'd have been halfway across the ocean—Amelia swallowed by the sea. What else could she rely on to make the choices she needed to make against the no? The no of convention, the no of record company executives, the no of those who valued the accumulation of money over raw joy, the no that wanted the world to stay exactly as it was because it profited from it—no matter that it destroyed so many lives, across generations, through conquest and domination. The mind was never simply the brain but something more interconnected and encompassing—she knew this better than anyone. Mind *was* body. Muscles were wisdom, the gut and nerves too. She believed there was a better way to live, not just with one another but with the earth: a realm unmapped, unseen. Getting "back to the garden" was never simply hippie lingo, even though some heard the song that way. It isn't easy to live with the idea that you're stardust, which was never meant to be figurative, a pretty line. The philosopher Teilhard de Chardin believed it to be truth.

How does your life change when you say yes to the truth?

I was dreaming, or in that hypnopompic fog in which I believed we were in some distant part of the world we'd never been to, some foggy island rather than a guest room in Provincetown, until I blinked. Jude still sleeping beside me. My vision hazy, grit in the corners, oily on the eyelids. I held up my phone, scrolling without intention.

Three posts down: *Joni Mitchell at the Newport Folk Festival.* I thought of the two times she'd appeared there: 1967 and 1969. I thought for sure that this was a reprise, some unearthed footage of a songwriters' workshop she'd done, Leonard Cohen, David Blue, Janis Ian, and Eric Andersen sharing the space on the stage, until I saw the date. July 24, 2022. I was still waking up. Last night. It had been last night?

Exhilaration. Excitement so hard and bright that it felt indistinguishable from pain—pain in the neck, pain all the way down into the fingertips—which is another way to say an excess of aliveness. Can you be so alive that the sky outside the window looks less like a sky than it does water? An ocean?

New England had turned itself inside out, as if I'd never spent any time here before.

I clicked on the video for "Both Sides Now." And in seconds the Joni I'd known was different, had altered, and not in the expected way. It wasn't simply that she was back to singing, and well. Instead, something of significance was happening, an alchemy. She was passing into her song; the song was sturdier than she was—even though it was very much Joni up there on a tufted rococo chair, looking straight at her audience or in some inscrutable distance, a radiance in creme and pale blue. This refraction was possible because the performers around her were being refracted too. Everyone was less singular because there wasn't a leader any longer. There was no center but a single organism from which parts radiated, a little like the wavering pink threads of a cell. Sometimes Joni's singing was in the foreground, sometimes the background. Now Brandi was in the foreground, then she fell out. And if a sustained note went flat, or words were forgotten, or a melodic leap didn't quite catch or reach its peak, it didn't so much matter. Someone was there to pick it up, hold it, and carry it along for the length of a line. Maybe that would be Joni, who appeared to be having the best time. The only child who finally knows the pleasure in having a troop of musical siblings, lots of nephews and nieces, an extended family of multiple generations.

I'd never seen the profound look so casual and fun.

A two-hour drive from Provincetown. Was she just waking up, the server rolling a room service tray through the door? Croissants, coffee, apricot jam in squat glass containers. Or had she already packed up hours ago, her plane already up at thirty-six thousand feet, over the Alleghenies?

Tributes had run their course by this point. This was more participatory, democratic. Equalized. Tribute flowed in one direction, but this put music in a whole new space, even though the space felt ancient, before money changed music, quantifying it, suppressing it. Money wasn't at the center of things. It was a campfire in which the songs themselves were the fire. Everyone had a chance to be the fire before passing along the ferro rod.

I was trying to be stoic but failing my test. I couldn't control the sounds of my crying any more than I could keep my face muscles still. And where had my sense of humor gone?

"Babe, what's wrong?" Jude said.

All I could manage was "Joni," and I pointed my phone at him. And soon the two of us were both tearing up. What was it? More life ahead of us, more than we thought we knew? We'd reconciled ourselves to losing her, and now she was back, sly thing. She'd always had plans to outsmart us—why should that have been such a shock? But the relief of it felt humbling, like the aftermath of a death, finding out a friend, family member, or beloved animal is gone. Cleansing tears, deep. As if you've touched the physical net of the body and felt the point at which you live, which is its own kind of joy.

We live in her time, and no one who comes after us will be able to say that.

We also live in a culture that throws older people away—I felt that immutably now, in my gut. We leave them facing the walls in their wheelchairs, we shut them in their rooms, or we don't even look at them—our faces go to everyone but theirs when they sit around the table. Imagine wiping them out to the point of offering a hello, a glance. But not this time. And this is what the world will look like if we put an end to a cruelty that goes unexamined because we are ashamed of ourselves, hate what experience does to a body, *our* bodies. If every single person who makes it to older age has such honor to look forward to.

Then there was "Shine," not quite the folk song of creation and destruction, the folk melody that wanted to hold them in the same space. Well, it was still that, but together the perfomers pulled its gospel roots out of the ground and were weaving

233

the plant of it in the air, blades dark purple-green, dirt flying all around. The late sun lighting up its grooves. And a singular vision went on after death, was that right? Joni had always set out to do that in her work, but now the action of that was already underway. And once the chair was empty, somebody else would sit down in it and warm it up until the next person took its place.

Music had gone out ahead of her, and she looked all around, as if startled over where the song had gone. She laughed, sometimes even in the middle of the song, which ended up lifting it in unexpected ways, both piercing the scrim of theater and bringing back a sense of play.

The becoming of thought, which doesn't move with a script and never knows which way it's going to go.

The story of edges and borders always a fiction.

"Write all that down," Jude said after I started to put my laptop away. "If you don't write it now, you're going to lose it all."

"Really?" I said. "Now? I have to write all this down now?"

"Yes," he smiled, certain that I'd know later what he meant.

So that is exactly what I did. Not inside the room, where he talked to his patients through his laptop for the next eight hours, but by myself, out on a chair pointed to the sun.

~~~~~

I was in Live Nation's ticket queue online. If I pictured it as an actual line of humans on a sidewalk outside a window, I loathed it a little less, but the internet turned even my anxiety into an abstraction, a condition my senses didn't know what to do with. "One thousand people ahead of you. Nine hundred people ahead of you.

Eight hundred fifty." I didn't know enough about high-demand concert events to know whether this text was pure manipulation or true to the metrics. The last performer of any stature I'd seen in concert was Tori Amos, whose ticket purchase was straightforward, as far as I remembered, no major dramas attached to it. I was competing with bots now. I sat in my office at school, my eyes fixing on numbers. I had to teach at two. It was thirty-five minutes to two.

At some point in the fall, it was announced that Joni was performing in Washington State on June 10, 2023. There was no question that Jude and I were going, though to say that had the arrogance of fantasy: *I'm going to make this happen.* Or *I'm going to make sure she's going to look at me from the stage.* Which would make me think, *Are you nuts?*, if I were hearing it from another person about someone who wasn't Joni.

I'd have had some container for this hunger if I hadn't had to teach that day. But the desire to be a good teacher and the desire to see Joni crashed up against each other. I wasn't able to bulkhead the two forces at once. They weren't opposed exactly, but they required different brains, different demeanors. One so feral that his eyes were a little wild, the other so dedicated to responsibility and integrity that he was practically an appliance. He could judge himself too thoroughly for not having an answer to a student question or for co-creating a fact from one of their essays, a posture that didn't feel terribly Joni, who, if she were a teacher, would probably sit at the head of the table and hold court by talking about her visits with Georgia O'Keeffe and Juan Hamilton rather than the stories submitted for workshop.

At one fifty-five p.m. I stomped and hurried past the library, across the campus, certain I'd lost my place in the queue. Certain that by closing my laptop, everything was finished now, and if I'd only had the courage of fidelity, I would have held the laptop in my outstretched hand as if protecting this signal was as crucial as protecting a line to the dead. I didn't want to look like an idiot. Easier to hold on to my belief that this was a doomed prospect; I didn't have the luck for this, maybe nobody did, unless you had Hollywood connections. Maybe that was it: maybe the entire audience would be filled with industry people—movie stars, other performers, managers, agents. The story already written before it played out. Chloë Sevigny in the front row.

Once I walked into my classroom, I opened my laptop. I was still in the queue—how could that be possible? Now twenty-five people ahead of me—could that be real? My students had already known I was writing a book about her; they were already excited about it, excited for me, not to mention Joni. Many began talking about their Joni connections in that way that Joni people do: *I'm closer to the work than you.* But the spirit was good in the room; it blew up competition and disrespect before it ever got the chance to rear its head. And then, miraculously, the queue was gone. I was floating now, snow in white space. There were no walls. No one ahead of me.

Time contracted like a snake about to strike. This was my window, my time. But the system stalled and sped up. Stalled and sped up again. I kept pushing a purchase key, and nothing happened. In the meantime I'd asked my student andie to introduce their piece and read the opening page. I wanted two different things too much. I scrolled for the few available options. Two tickets, close to a month's rent. The word *privilege* swiped into my skull while the memory of my father's face scoffed at me. My father. He'd drive ten miles out of the way in order to bypass a fifty-cent toll bridge because he'd grown up poor and couldn't ever shake the dust of that money anxiety out of his head.

And then?

A breath in the room. Everything seemed to stop. The light rail out the window—stop. Even the cars on Cooper Street.

Sterling-Elizabeth, Sienna, andie, Juliet, Miriam, Esther, Adam, Jade, Jennifer, David, Brandon, Betsy. It felt like it was as much their moment as it was mine. We were making it together, when the point of it was less about the object than it was the chord we had struck, which wasn't too neat, wasn't resolved. It rang like a sound we'd always want to go back to. We missed it already.

"Fuck yeah!" I cried, punching the air over my head. And tenth row from the stage—what?

Clapping. The whole room. In my head I thanked the class for giving that moment to me. Whatever was there about glitch and belief, the two combined. We all laughed, hard. And, with one deep breath, I did what I could to center myself while we proceeded to get down to examples of sensory language in andie's essay.

But not before I texted, *Babe, we're going to Washington!*

~~~~~

Seven months later Jude and I were walking through the woods of Seattle's Discovery Park. Our desire to explore had won out over our depletion. We'd both gotten to the airport before dawn to make our flights. I was marveling at the fact that an actual forest, brambly and not too tended, could thrive within a city's borders, only a six-mile drive from its downtown streets. Exhaustion had tipped me over into a bit of a dream state, which meant that for minutes at a time, I'd forget that we were here in the city to get our bearings, and we'd be driving southeast across the mountains to see Joni in three days.

"There's an owl up ahead," a woman whispered, approaching from the opposite direction. "On the path to the left. Look up on the branch."

We rushed forward but were quiet about it. And not so high above us perched the creature, larger than I would have imagined, the size of the largest household cat. So many streaks of colors that it looked designed. Tan, gray, brown, ruddy brown, white, as intricate as a sweater on a display table in East Hampton.

The owl looked down at us, unbothered by our cameras, our talking. After a minute it rotated its head to the right while keeping its body in the same direction, as if just to show us it could do it. But I am already giving the owl human traits. The owl was both immediate and otherworldly, with a face that looked as benevolent as it did inscrutable. An aura of calm anesthetized the air from around the owl, which felt like a part of its doing, even though a blue jay kept shrieking all but ten feet away. The owl was not to be moved, even when I walked directly beneath him, and Jude took my picture.

The owl's eyes. Spacious. Dark. Deep. They could have gone all the way to the other side of the sea.

~~~

The outdoor temperature falling: forty-nine, forty-eight, forty-seven. Rain pounding the windshield. Mist rising up the mountain slopes, through the evergreens, as the pickup dipped down another slope. Wasn't it supposed to be a sunny day, highs near eighty? Well, we still had a long way past the other side of the Cascades. A high desert spiked with sagebrush lay on the other side, at least according to the guidebook I'd read.

On my last drive to a Joni concert, I thought for sure some calamity would happen along the way. An accident on Route 6 by the South Dennis exit, a bomb blowing up the suspended deck of the Sagamore Bridge. An obstacle preventing us from reaching the venue in Boston's Seaport District. This time none of that. The clock, and all its pressures, fell away. We were in the desert, which flattened time. Basalt cliffs as far as the eye could see. Our hands clasped across the black console of the pickup.

~~~~~

By the time we reached our seats, we'd passed through several portals that felt like they'd taken days: the line to get in the parking lot, the line to present tickets, the line to buy T-shirts, the line to get lemonade, the line to find our seats, the line to the porta-potty. Perhaps there's something conscious about all this by design. By the time the viewer finds their place for the next three hours, they are porous, pliable, too tired to revolt, and ready to receive any signals without complaint.

We were close to the stage but to the left. Right in front of a screen that intended to magnify the stage for all twenty-seven thousand audience members, most of whom sat on the grass in lawn chairs or blankets. Equipment blocked the center of the stage from our vantage point. Was that going to be a problem for us?

Would we be *at* the concert but viewing the concert through another frame? Had we come all this way for an experience we could have watched on our laptops at a Provincetown guesthouse as we had with Newport?

Already the light of the screen was dyeing our faces bright orange.

~~~~~

As soon as I settled into my seat, something overtook me, not so much having to do with myself but with the man seated to my left, holding my hand. I thought of the chain of events that had led Jude to this concert, which had started long before we'd even gotten together. His years in med school in San Diego, when he fell in love with Joni's music for the first time while looking at the eucalyptus leaves outside his apartment window. His years in residency in Atlanta, when he sang "Same Situation" in his car late at night after having been awake for another thirty-two-hour shift. Sitting in the audience for Joni's seventy-fifth birthday celebration at Dorothy Chandler Pavilion. Sitting in the orchestra loft for Brandi's *Blue* concert and seeing Joni's face and body language across the stage. Alone in his Huntington Beach studio apartment after the ending of his long relationship, at the start of the pandemic, with the kind of time on his hands that he'd never had before, trying to sing and play one of Joni's songs. It wasn't that he hadn't tried before, he told me. He'd tried and given up many times over the years, even though he could perform dozens of other songs. Anyone who's tried to play her work knows how forbidding it can be on ten levels at once, but it finally clicked when he sang "Blue" for about the two hundredth time, the performance of which he'd sent to me. He looked into my face as he sang each line, believing it were indeed possible to look into someone's face through the footprint of a phone.

And here we were together. We'd transformed our digital lives into skin, his shoulder leaning into my shoulder. I didn't believe in the idea of fate, not because I was inclined to disbelieve it but because life always felt more inscrutable to me than fate—elastic, unpredictable, harder to pin down. And here we were together. We'd been practicing for each other all our lives but hadn't known it till now. All the relationships that had ended, chastening, bewildering us? *Practicing.* Heartbreak shearing off thirty pounds of me over one summer, even though I was still eating and hadn't done one thing to change my diet? Practicing. For that knowledge to settle in, simultaneous, changed, *charged* my sense of identity. I wasn't only myself anymore. Jude wasn't either, and this happened among others, alongside them. By this point we'd been together for eighteen months, through ten states, from Vermont to Mississippi to California, though no night together had felt as—manifold. For the first time I was in my life and not hovering above my life. I loved him to the point of speechlessness. The sunset flared in the sky beyond the stage.

~~~~~

And then we were in the concert, which is another way to say we were way out in the sea: boundless, pushed around by waves, dust gone. Joni sat far back from the edge of the stage in a semicircle of chairs, and from our tenth-row seats, she was obscured by all the equipment needed to pull off the event. Instead, we saw her on the screen, magnified, as large as a five-story building. Again she'd managed to wear an outfit that was meant to be iconic. The expected beret, expected glasses tinted halfway up the lens, but this time a red patterned silk shirt that moved like a sail every time a gust blew up from the gorge. At Newport she'd worn sturdier fabric, but now she didn't need that external skin; her sturdiness was coming through her voice. This outfit would influence the next three hours, the image of her setting the mood as much as that *Clouds* cover had when I saw it at eight years old.

The first song? "Big Yellow Taxi." I told myself beforehand that it was going to be okay if the concert stayed in this realm. This wasn't safety on her part, though it was easy to mistake it as such. In fact, Jude had already told me plenty about recovery from a neurologist's perspective. Recovery from a brain injury is one of the longest arcs in clinical medicine—eventually the organ merges into new ways of learning and compensating. Another way to put it: when you can't do a task, you find another way to do it, literally blazing a new brain circuit. This can take years. There often simply isn't enough time if you're older, and when you indeed make progress, it's often quite slow, too slow for anyone to recognize. For all these reasons, I'd already decided before the concert that it was too much to want a new song or even hope for a reach into the catalogue, a deep cut or two. But the second song was "Night Ride Home," a song that could have been a hit but probably sounded retro in the confused culture of 1991, torn between gloss and grunge. Not the most obvious choice but the perfect choice, as it captured the roadsides we'd all driven through to get here, the grapevines trellised with their catch wires and end-post assemblies. Hit, deep cut, hit, as much as any Joni song could be called a hit. Or a deep cut, for that matter. What is a deep cut when deep cuts comprised the body of her work? The very metaphor prioritized the hit, and once again a different language needed to be applied to Joni.

~~~~

I took in some songs, others not as much as I wanted to, though there was never a second in which I didn't feel magnetized. There was "Raised on Robbery," brought back to its roots as a blues song once its Andrews Sisters harmonies were clipped away. There was "Come In From The Cold," a song I thought I was supposed to like more than I actually did, maybe because the "we" of it seemed to be speaking for a generation I didn't exactly belong to but was close enough to see. Or was it about the music? I didn't like the music, the production; it didn't excite me, didn't vary enough from verse to verse. But now I *heard* and felt it. The musicians found the emotion in it. It wasn't just Joni pushing her voice higher than her natural register or the quiet of the instruments on the verse about value judgments. It was the way the voices—Joni, Brandi, and Taylor Goldsmith—threaded and built upon one another in dialogue. The "we" of the song was no longer a theory, but a "we" enacted. I felt them thinking together, insight upon insight, and the emotional responsibility of the song could be divided, a shared thing.

When Joni began "Amelia," I knew her singing was one key lower than the guitar chord. I didn't know how this would change, but by the second verse she'd climbed to the plateau where the instrumentalists had been waiting for her, though not so much that they'd lagged or looked over their shoulders in concern. They all went forward in sync, moving with confidence now. To feel that shift was to listen to someone learn how to walk all over again, but this time the footsteps were sound.

~~~~~

I've always loved "Help Me," but it isn't a representative Joni song, if such a thing is even possible. Rather, it's a representative song of its age, in that musically it can sit between Stevie Wonder and Steely Dan. Its subject is sexual freedom—especially sexual freedom for women—and the anxiety that comes with the possibility of coupling. Joni's collaborator Celisse Henderson sang it in a way that cracked the song open, playing up the contrast between the verses and the chorus. She sang the verses accompanied by her guitar. At the chorus, the congas joined in, the bass, another guitar, and Mark Isham's trumpet. The performance then dramatized the tension between sexual exploration and monogamy. It did so in a way that was playful, smart, and sexy, especially because it left so many gaps—the longing!—in the final verse. Joni appeared to be awed, and she turned toward Celisse with a beaming face as Celisse laughed back, stomping the floor with her shoes. What else do you do when Joni's face telegraphs such vibrancy?

Four songs later Wendy Melvoin sang "A Strange Boy," which talks back to "Help Me." Imagine the speaker of the latter, a few years older now, thinking about the costs of that freedom, especially after breaking up with someone who refused to grow up, someone she'd given her power over to. What kept this song vibrant wasn't just Wendy's vocals but the way she still graciously held on to the song in spite of Joni's attempts to both join in and . . . maybe take it back? (*I wrote that song. And not only that, I remember the words—all of them!*) Its greatest trait was the rhythm, driving, foregrounded, in contrast to the more restrained original. By emphasizing the beat, the performance was honoring all of Joni's experiments with rhythm, from "Lucky Girl" to "Turbulent Indigo" to "This Place." It was the groove that kept the song's persistent brooding eros at its center. The rhythm never let you forget what it was really about, what its drama was in reaction to; it was no wonder that some of the other musicians rose to their feet. In the quietest way, Prince had been brought back into the space. Prince, who had hired Wendy & Lisa as collaborating musicians because, as Wendy recalled in her introduction, they "sounded like Joni Mitchell."

After that? "Cactus Tree," excellent sequence. Led by Jess Wolfe and Holly Laessig of Lucius, joined by Celisse and Brandi. During the performance, Joni mostly kept her face down. Was she resting? Tired of the sound and lights in her eyes? While listening to previous performances, she'd tapped her bear-head cane as if it were a processing tool, the means through which she took in rhythm. Now, there was a cloud about her, a silence. I had a notion that the song felt new to her all over again, and she was trying to recall what had driven her to write it. The archive of men whom she had been drawn to or vice versa, but not so much that she had been ready to give up her freedom. How young she'd been. Was she thinking about those men? Trying to remember each one's face and hands, how they might have looked at her and turned away when confounded by her resolve? When the song ended, she lifted her head, face gleaming, a grin. She looked all around at the singers as if thanking them. Her reaction opened yet another door, and I wanted to hear the song again.

~~~~~

The performance of "Shine" was a foregone conclusion, especially because Brandi had openly called it one of her favorite Joni Mitchell songs and had just performed it again for the Gershwin Prize broadcast. I'm not sure any version of "Shine" could match the version I'd heard from Newport, which took off like an idea bearing fruit in real time, a short denim skirt reimagined as a floor-length gospel gown, which needed an audience to make it happen. Every note felt inhabited and full of conviction, but this version might have already been too sure of itself by now. The script was in place, and it hadn't yet realized that there were more versions to come, and that this one was just on the way. Maybe that gospel element needed to be threaded with the unlikely, an unexpected fabric. It was now stitched inside a genre, and the best of Joni's songs always bind multiple genres.

So what tore it open wasn't Joni or Brandi but the audience. Jude and I looked over our shoulders to see twenty-seven thousand people waving cell phone flashlights behind us. That might have seemed old hat at any other stadium-sized concert but for this song, this night. Maybe we all sensed it would be new to Joni, who hadn't performed outside at night in twenty-three years, years before the iPhone had made its debut. This time *we* were the performers; we were giving something back, and by the end, she asked Brandi, "Where did they get the lights?"

"Cell phones," Brandi said.

"Cell phones!" Joni said, laughing, a little awkward, no doubt thinking of the swipe the song had just taken against those "busy talking on their cell phones."

"You look like a fallen constellation," she said, in correction. "You are stardust." Everyone laughed, though not missing the point at its mysterious core. We put our phones back in our pockets.

~~~~

I didn't think my sensory apparatus could handle any more. One could only be a struck tuning fork for so long before the vibrations started turning in on themselves, and it was impossible to hear those waves. Newport had been eleven songs, an hour and one minute exactly. And within minutes we'd be near the three-hour mark. By which I mean close to midnight. I was already thinking of the hour walk back to the parking lot, the hour crawling through the vineyards to I-90, the hour-plus drive up 97 to Peshastin, where we'd be laying down our heads—by dawn most likely. Sky full of light if there wasn't a mountain blocking it. There was the requisite "Both Sides Now" and "The Circle Game." Encores were to come, but the question was, how many? This audience wasn't going to let go of her if it was up to them. I imagined the clapping being heard all the way to Seattle or high enough up to enter a cockpit. The pilot flying solo east to Providence, Rhode Island.

Halfway through Newport, a guitar had been handed to Joni, and she'd played the chord patterns of "Just Like This Train" as an instrumental, leaning up against the piano. This time she was doing the same thing but sitting down. I was thinking about what it took to learn her instrument. It was said that she'd watched videos of herself on YouTube. The younger self teaching the older self how to make the chord shapes again. It was still remarkable to behold the ease with which she played, the way she leaned into the guitar's body as if it had always been an extension of her rib cage, the two never having been separated. There was no look of excessive absorption on her face, no compressed lips or frown. She was down inside the interior space from which music lifts.

And the biggest turn of the night, the joy of the night? A string of chords, minor chords, modal, lush, menacing, like harmony re-cast and heard through a head cold, if a head cold could come with some use aside from its downright aggravations. The song "If," her setting of Rudyard Kipling's poem, a song no one seemed to rec-ognize. She was not only playing but singing, voice box and hands moving in unison. The physical feat of that turned a spotlight on the song, a song that had gone out into the world without much notice. Earlier in the night Brandi had asked Joni what her favorite song was, and she'd said, "If." Rudyard Kipling. And what little awkwardness there was—silence expanding the air between them like a thought bubble—seemed to be about several things at once. The expectation that Joni mention a song that wasn't her own. And Rudyard Kipling—wasn't there something unpleasant, problem-atic about his work, that name? ("Jingo imperialist," Orwell had written. "Morally insensitive and aesthetically disgusting.") But maybe Joni had picked the song because imperialism wasn't in its atmosphere—she'd found Kipling at his most generous. The song itself was so idiosyncratic, so little known, that it made "A

Strange Boy," thus far the most adventurous outing of the night, sound like a Top 40 hit. And in that way, among this community of musicians that had become so beloved to her, Joni was taking herself back, which had always been the hardest choice, a deeper life lesson to pass on to us than any moment that had happened all night. It was so easy to present the comprehensible Joni, and lately she'd been willing to go along because that's what people wanted; that's what made them flower. But even if you didn't want to come along with the full song, there was always the sinewy adhesion of those bulky chords, the pulsing of one particular body moving through time and space with worn-out tools.

~~~~

When I was child, you could have told me, *Sit down there*, pointing to the mud, and I would have done it. Climb up the side of that garbage pile? I'd have done that too. *Sign this, wear this, take off your clothes, put them back on, run this mile, then do it backward.* It hadn't occurred to me that I could say no, as ridiculous as that sounds. I might say that I took in the lessons of obedience taught by my parents, school, and church, and took them in a little too far, took them to an extreme, but is that the whole story? Later, in the years right after high school, a friend of mine tried to strong-arm me into signing up for a training program that was supposed to transform your personality through teaching you to de-emphasize emotion in favor of reason. I knew it was scam, possibly even a cult, and each time I wrenched my head to the left, over the period of an hour or more, I knew I was saying no for my life. I refused to sign on. My friend loved me but was drawn to me in part because I must have looked like someone who was easy to push around. When some see that quality in a person—whether it is in their gestures, the way they shape their vowels, their tendency to redden and smile and agree and give the best of themselves—they want to hurt that person as a way to dominate, a way to feel their power all the way down to their feet. It is primal. Think of a lion being drawn to an antelope, the fresh meat of that creature by the road, steaming.

Still. There was blank space at the center of me, in spite of my no to my friend. Joni's *Dog Eat Dog* had come out around that time, and I played the song "Fiction" constantly at the expense of just about all the other songs until that part of the record was scratchy from use, because that song knew something. It knew about the culture's tendency to amplify dangerous impulses to fiery needs, and though it simply sounded like a register of oppositions, a list of culturally constructed absurdities, it wanted to dramatize what it felt like to live without a center, some mechanism in your particular body that told you, *No, this is wrong. This could eat you alive.* It knew how vulnerable to coercion the structures we built made us.

Which invariably suggested that there was another way to live on the other side of that no, if you were willing to put in the hard work. Maybe your creative work was the channel through which you inhabited that vision, again and again, day after day. For someone else it could be teaching, social justice, working in medicine—anything that could thwart all that was wrong with the world. All the suffering and indifference you wanted to change and make better.

I'm afraid to say Joni's songs saved my life, because it sounds too easy, but then again, no—I'll break through that wall. Those songs did save my life. They showed me that you could take what others saw as awkwardness, limitation—*failure*—an aspect of ridicule, and spin it into pure gold. The songs knew that this gold was irreplaceable, a substance ten times more powerful than habit, all the rote, mechanized ways we move through the calendar from one day to the next. They knew something about the hard, enduring pleasures of difficulty, of throwing out the old plans and making something new out of the broken pieces, again and again. They trusted in bewilderment, in a line-by-line path of discovery, in which the song tried to find itself, *become* itself through the process of testing, thinking, going the unexpected route. As for ease of production, ease of engagement, ease as a goal, the force the tech giants expect us to champion in this age? The songs knew that ease is a deceptive god, only destined to exhaust and drain us and steal our delight.

Here's to delight.

~~~~

I'm always drawn to the air and light of early summer, but this time of year collides with the anniversaries of my parents' deaths, a realization that always comes to me by the end of June, days too late to be sorrowful. What do I miss most about them? Their voices. I never made videos of them when they were still around because I'd assumed, mistakenly, that pictures would be enough, that a more complete representation of them would only magnify their inevitable loss. The one reason I delay turning my air conditioner on every summer is not for any love of heat or humidity but the sounds of voices from outside: sparrow chat, intricate conversations about co-op boards, children calling out to their friends, dogs mimicking sirens. Once the air conditioner goes on, the apartment feels sterile, sealed off from the smells of Canadian wildfires and weed smoke up from the sidewalk—in other words, all the hot mess of life, the noise, the stink, and it is no longer the fourth floor of a Brooklyn brownstone, even though I still have the same address.

And now it occurs to me that what I love most about the people I am close to is the sounds of their voices. Jude's voice. Baritone, from low in his chest, a rich violet clay with streaks of sandstone, which always conjures up his whole body for me, even if his body is right there beside me, leg pressed into my leg. "You okay, babe?" he says. And his right hand grips my left hand tighter, which I never grow tired of.

I wouldn't be telling you the full truth if I didn't say I missed all the other Joni voices. The voice that poured from her tonight was richer, nimbler, more nuanced than her Newport voice. Out of nowhere she'd sing a phrase so anguished and full of longing, it would shake the song off its original foundation, and the whole audience would respond to it, bodily, at once. (*There you are! You're back.*) But on other songs, her voice could stray off pitch at times: amelodic. It wasn't always in negotiation with the beat, which didn't always align with the tap of her cane. It couldn't conjure up pictures like it once had, wavering a sustained vowel to imply moonlight on water. My desire to cheer her on felt a little like a drug in that its euphoria kept getting in the way of my seeing truth. (*You're all better now, right? You've never sounded better.*) That drug wanted to believe in resurrection. That drug wanted to believe that obstacles were surmountable, that anyone could come back from disaster and not simply come back, but be richer for the test. The complexity of that rush was as much about me as it was Joni, until I realized that none of this was about Joni, defender of oppositions, contradictions, the in-between. In truth, I didn't want to be reminded that the body has an ending, or that I have an ending, or that this book does as well, or any of the people who sat in front of and alongside me, even those who were mildly exasperating in their efforts to perform their connections to Joni. When I let that in, I felt myself wilt from inside, both heartbroken and frozen in a region of self that I often didn't have access to. I wanted joy to light me up like a torch. I wanted this night to soar, just like everyone else did in these chairs. It took so much to get here. A return or a farewell? To ignore the possibility of an ending was to fail to see. It was a disservice to all the changes Joni still had ahead of her.

By midnight Jude and I ended up in the throng walking toward the narrow gate of the exit, singing in full voice to "All I Want." The "lonely road." Maybe twenty-seven thousand people were joining in with the sound system as they walked out through the closed-down concessions into the night. It felt like being a pilgrim, which made me laugh, because that's the last thing Joni would have wanted to be, another cult of personality. But it was no longer about her songs as much as it was living the best we could in the moment, and I imagined the procession of us falling at the end of a movie or seen from forty feet up in the air by an owl. Individual voices as candles awaiting their extinction. I was struck by how unselfconscious I felt in my singing after all this time silent. Thirty years? My self-consciousness, as it often did, went first to pitch, but twelve notes in, my larynx opened up like a trap with a hinge, and I was too immersed in the shape of the melody to care very much about sounding wrong. Together we were making one thing. Dozens of us. And it didn't matter that I'd messed up that word or that we hadn't picked up dinner in Ellensburg or that my throat felt a little raw from all the notes I'd aimed high over the security fence.

~~~~

I didn't know that it was possible to walk in inch-deep snow and feel the seventy-two-degree heat on my arms, but there we were, fourteen hours after the final encore, with Mount Rainier closer than I'd ever expected to see it. I took a picture of Jude. Jude took a picture of me, with melting snow, sunlight, a winding stream in the background. Snow sloppy, glacial, almost sky blue. Earlier I had thought I needed grounding, recovery, a whole day lying around under the covers in the Wenatchee, but now it was clear that anything less than a mountaintop would have been insufficient. 14,410 feet above sea level. "That mountain," Jude said, not taking his eyes off it. "When does it stop? It's endless. It's like looking into an owl's eyes." And there, already in memory, was another Rainier, corporeal and in miniature, so light that it could perch on a branch overhanging a path and fly off in absolute silence when the planet got too hot to bear. And then I thought that it was like seeing Joni last night—*Was it only last night?*—looking up at the bright screen towering in front of us, our necks tense with trying to take all of her in. Both young and old, male and female, more mountain than human, which didn't intend to take her vulnerability away or turn her into ice or stone. How could we, with such a colossal view of her moving hands and face? As sublime as she was, the new Joni had roots, the deepest roots. She was incredibly down-to-earth. Ready to laugh, too evolved for awkwardness to be of any concern, and grateful for all the thanks extended to her in a husky, burnished voice that sounded like she didn't take a single second of life for granted. Not one second. She wanted to be with us. She chose to.

ACKNOWLEDGMENTS

THIS BOOK BEGAN AS AN HOMAGE TO THE SONGS OF JONI MITCHELL, and it soon became that, and more: a thank you to the people who helped to shape my creative life. Some of them appear in the pages of this book; some are offstage, which doesn't mean they're not inside its cadences and descriptions. Someday I must find a way to make a book that has the capacity to feature everyone!

My editor Rakesh Satyal knew that I should write this story before I did. I'm so grateful for his vision, guidance, and scrupulous eye. Permission, too—no small thing coming from another deep Joni fan, whose own Joni is likely different from my Joni. I'll always be grateful to him for making a home for this book.

I also want to thank Ryan Amato and everyone at HarperOne for the attention and integrity they've channeled into this book's production.

Thanks, too, to my agent, Matt McGowan, for his good stewardship over the years and for taking good care of this project at all its junctures.

Thank you to Kathy Daneman for always being in my court. Thank you, too, to everyone on the PR team at HarperOne.

Thank you to Leslie Shipman and the people at The Shipman Agency for their kindness and support.

To all my students over the years—thank you! My fellow writers—thank you, too! You challenge me to be better in all ways.

To my dearest Elizabeth McCracken, friend, brilliant writer, and reader: I love you.

My comrades, past, present, and future: Anna deVries, Fiona McCrae, Alyson Sinclair, and Michael Taeckens.

Jude Theriot came into my life two weeks before I began writing this manuscript. "Love came to my door," as Joni sings, and our connection happened as spontaneously as the reach of that phrase. He read this book through its multiple drafts, listened to me, offered suggestions and encouragement, wished the best for me, made me laugh, and held my hand—literally. His spirit infuses these pages. Every word of this book is for him.

After the toughest days of the pandemic, it felt necessary to be out among other people, and I want to acknowledge the public places in which I worked on early drafts, where the rhythms of human speech and the sound of shoes against the floor felt like life again. To the librarians and workers at the Brooklyn Public Library (Cadman Plaza West), Brooklyn, New York; Montauk Library, Montauk, New York; George W. Armstrong Library, Natchez, Mississippi; and the Provincetown Public Library, Provincetown, Massachusetts—thank you. To the workers at these coffee bars for their sustenance and good spirit: The Art of the Bean and Leaf, Asbury Park, New Jersey; Brooklyn Roasting Company (Clinton Street), Brooklyn, New York; CC's

Coffee House, New Iberia, Louisiana; French Truck (Magazine Street), New Orleans, Louisiana; Joe (Hicks Street), Brooklyn, New York; Locals Collective NYC, Arverne by the Sea, New York; Panther Coffee (Biscayne Boulevard), Miami, Florida; Rêve Coffee Roasters (Rue Jefferson), Lafayette, Louisiana; The Studio Gallery and Coffee Bar, St. Martinville, Louisiana; the late Wired Puppy, Provincetown, Massachusetts.

Thank you, finally, to the Returning Residency and Summer Project Residency Programs at the Fine Arts Work Center in Provincetown for the gifts of space and time.

ABOUT THE AUTHOR

〰〰〰〰〰

PAUL LISICKY IS THE AUTHOR OF *Lawnboy, Famous Builder, The Burning House, Unbuilt Projects, The Narrow Door: A Memoir of Friendship*, and *Later: My Life at the Edge of the World*. His work has appeared in *The Atlantic, BuzzFeed, Conjunctions, The Cut, Fence, Foglifter, The New York Times Book Review, The Offing*, and *Ploughshares*, among other magazines and anthologies. A graduate of the Iowa Writers' Workshop, he has held fellowships from the John Simon Guggenheim Memorial Foundation, the National Endowment for the Arts, and the Fine Arts Work Center in Provincetown, where he has served on the writing committee since 2000. He received the Rose Dorothea Award from the Provincetown Public Library in 2022. He has taught in the creative writing programs at Cornell University, New York University, Sarah Lawrence College, and the University of Texas at Austin, as well as in the Bread Loaf Writers' Conference, the Tin House Summer and Winter Workshops, and the Juniper Summer Writing Institute. He is currently a professor of English in the MFA program at Rutgers University–Camden, where he is the editor of *StoryQuarterly*. He lives in Brooklyn.